TERAH KATHRYN COLLINS

HOME DESIGN WITH

Feng Shui

A-Z

Hay House, Inc.
Carlsbad, California · Sydney, Australia

LIFE
Styles

Published and distributed in the United States by: Hay House, Inc., P.O. Box 5100, Carlsbad, CA 92018-5100 • (800) 654-5126 • (800) 650-5115 (fax)

Edited by: Jill Kramer   *Designed by:* Christy Salinas

Library of Congress Cataloging-in-Publication Data

Collins, Terah Kathryn
    Home design with feng shui A–Z   /   Terah Kathryn Collins.
            p.   cm.
    ISBN 1-56170-572-1 (hardcover) • 1-56170-788-0 (tradepaper)
    1.   Feng-shui.   I.   Title.
BF1779.F4C64   1999
133.3'337—dc21   98-36480
                                                   CIP

ISBN 1-56170-788-0

04 03 02 01   12 11 10 9
1st printing, January 1999
9th printing, September 2001

Printed in China through Palace Press International

Contents

Introduction

In 1989, I fell passionately in love with Feng Shui (pronounced *FUNG SHWAY*) while listening to Feng Shui expert Dr. Richard Tan speak on the subject in San Diego. Now, ten years later, as a practitioner, author, speaker, and teacher of Feng Shui, my interest in the subject is continually piqued by the positive effects it has on people's lives, including my own. My studies with Dr. Tan, Louis Audet, Master Lin Yun, and many others, along with my experiences working with thousands of homes and offices, have inspired me to develop *Essential Feng Shui*. While honoring the essence of Feng Shui's Eastern heritage, I find immense value in focusing on the many *practical* benefits and applications Essential Feng Shui can bring to our Western culture.

This practical focus offers a clear pathway to transformation. As my clients enhance their environments, all kinds of positive results occur in their lives. Careers ignite, relationships heal, prosperity grows, and creativity soars.

The benefits of Feng Shui have certainly been evident in my life since the day I began practicing. Among them was the meeting and marrying of my soulmate, Brian Collins; finding a home that is our personal paradise; and meeting Louise Hay, the woman who encouraged me to write and who then went on to publish my first book, *The Western Guide to Feng Shui*.

I poured my heart and soul into that book, and the stories of my Feng Shui experiences tumbled out. In return, I was showered with letters and calls from readers all over the world requesting information on classes and consultations. To answer the call, I founded the Western School of Feng Shui to provide consultations and education in Essential Feng Shui. In 1997, as the school was taking its first steps, I wrote and recorded *The Western Guide to Feng Shui* six-tape audio program to complement and expand upon my book. In 1998, with the school in full swing, I immersed myself in writing my upcoming book, *The Western Guide to Feng Shui—Room by Room* (to be published by Hay House in February 1999). "But before you complete that," Hay House suggested, "why don't you write a quick reference guide that makes Feng Shui easily accessible to everyone." My practical nature loved the idea, and *Home Design with Feng Shui A–Z* jumped into the front seat of my trusty laptop.

Now, as it leaves my office and enters the world, I send it with this blessing: *May this book's contents, and the spirit in which it was written, put you in the command position of your own life's journey.*

After all, that's where you belong.

— Terah Kathryn Collins

How to Use This Book

The purpose of this book is to help you find the answers to your Feng Shui questions as quickly and easily as possible without having to wade through any extraneous material. If you are designing your dining room, look under "D" for practical Feng Shui suggestions on dining rooms. It's as simple as that.

You will also find listings such as History of Feng Shui and Philosophy of Feng Shui, as well as those on specific enhancements such as Plants, Crystals, and Water Features. These are cross-referenced to take you on a fact-finding journey that will specifically meet your needs and enrich your knowledge and enjoyment of Feng Shui.

As a holistic art and science, Feng Shui addresses both your inner and outer domain. As you read this book, you will find that most listings include "Inner Work," which explores the thoughts and feelings that complement your outer Feng Shui enhancements. To fully experience the transformative power that Feng Shui can have in your life, I highly recommend that you work with both the inner and outer suggestions.

Home Design with Feng Shui A–Z is a buffet of sorts, where you can taste or feast on Feng Shui as you wish. Enjoy the cornucopia of information, and may it give you all the sustenance you need to create your own personal paradise.

The A-Z List

ANGLES AND CORNERS

In Feng Shui, where safety and comfort are paramount, protruding sharp angles and corners are considered dangerous. They produce "cutting Ch'i" (pronounced *CHEE*), or arrowlike energy that can make people feel irritable, uncomfortable, and unsafe (see Ch'i, page 36). Our angular Western architecture also creates corners in every room where Ch'i tends to collect and stagnate. In Feng Shui, these extreme features need to be balanced.

Even if the general shape is square or rectangular, choose architectural designs and furniture with rounded corners and more organic lines to assure safety and comfort.

When existing furniture has sharp corners, drape fabric or a vining plant over the corners to soften them, or turn furniture at a diagonal to minimize the corner's effect.

Balance protruding angles with the softening influence of plants, screens, textiles, and lighting. Or explore the magical possibilities of faux painting and *trompe l'oeil* (a French term meaning "to fool the eye").

Fill in room corners with items that soften and round them out, such as lamps, curtains, plants, baskets, screens, art, and diagonally placed furniture.

INNER WORK—*Are there any sharp edges or dark corners within you? Do you feel "edgy," irritated, or cornered in some way? Once you've identified an inner "poison arrow," soften and disarm it with compassion and forgiveness. Let go of any hard and fast position, and consider positive outcomes where everyone wins. Dissolve edginess with "soft" activities such as soaking in a hot bath, relaxing by a warm fire, or taking a nature walk. Know that you can always balance inner-cutting Ch'i by doing something for yourself that is nurturing and kind.*

Once you've identified an inner "poison arrow," soften and disarm it with compassion and forgiveness.

ANIMALS

When loved and well cared for, animals are natural batteries of lively Ch'i. As is always the case in Feng Shui, the key to success is care. Treat your animal companions with love and dignity, and they will "spark" your life.

 Make sure indoor pets have their own special place in your home. Dogs and cats need a bed, rug, or mat that's specifically theirs. Smaller animals need their own cages or tanks that give them plenty of room to live happy, healthful lives.

 Keep pet homes fresh and clean to assure the health and vitality of your animals, as well as the quality of Ch'i flowing through your home. Don't allow anyone—child or adult—to abuse or neglect a pet, and pay close attention to the well-being of pets living in children's rooms.

 If your pets live outdoors, they also need clean, dry homes and places to exercise. Dog runs and horse stables need to be large and cleared of manure every day.

The best remedy for cat and rabbit litter boxes is to keep them extra clean. Keep them hooded and out of the way in garages, large bathrooms, or basements.

ART

Art of all kinds, including paintings, sculptures, collages, and textiles, has a powerful effect on people. To enhance the Ch'i in your home, choose art that elicits positive feelings and in some way makes your heart sing. Your goal is to make sure that every piece of art in your home is one that you love.

 Match your art with the function of each room. Choose soothing, romantic, or sensual art for your bedroom; lively, colorful art for the living room; and powerful, motivational art for your home office.

 Use the Bagua Map (page 131) to help you find the places in your home that correlate with your goals in life. If you want romance and your Love and Marriage area is in the dining room, choose art that's romantic and appropriate for your dining area. If you wish to improve your health, and your Health and Family area is in the bathroom, display art there that evokes radiant health and vitality.

 Honor everyone living with you by making sure they also like the art displayed in shared rooms.

Choose art that elicits positive feelings.

 Your art should portray whole images and serene or inspirational subject matter. Art depicting violence, death, distortion, or negativity is not recommended.

 Very special Ch'i resides in art that you and your family create. Sow your personal Ch'i into your home by expressing your creativity. Make sure you aren't hiding away any art pieces that deserve to be framed and displayed.

INNER WORK—*Look at the art you have in your home now. What is each piece "saying" to you? Is it inspiring you or depressing you; affirming or scolding you? Learn from its voice, and then decide whether it should remain in your life. If it doesn't belong with you anymore, let it go by trading, selling, or giving it away.*

Everything kept in attics and basements should be loved or useful.

ATTICS AND BASEMENTS

Attics and basements, like all storage areas, need to be organized (see Philosophy of Feng Shui, page 105). Everything kept there should be loved or useful in some way. Be sure to give everything you own *a good home* that's easily accessible, uncluttered, and well lit.

INNER WORK—*Attics and basements are often a study of what you are holding on to from the past. Ask yourself why you are keeping these things. As you look through the items stored in your attic or basement, think about what, or who, they represent. Do the memories weaken or strengthen you? Is it time to let them go? Or, is it time to dust them off and bring them out where you can really enjoy them?*

BATHROOMS

The primary function of our bathrooms is to cleanse our bodies—inside and out—via the sink, shower, bathtub, and toilet. In Feng Shui, plumbing is considered a potential threat to the vital Ch'i circulating through the house. Just like water, Ch'i can be pulled down the drain. Although we're grateful to have bathrooms so conveniently located in our homes, we certainly don't want to flush our prosperity down the toilet or watch our health go down the drain! We can design our bathrooms so that the Ch'i remains buoyant; and our health, wealth, and happiness flourish.

Keep the drains of the tub and sink closed when not in use, and make sure you keep the lid on the toilet seat closed. The latter is especially important due to the toilet's large opening.

If possible, install the toilet so that you don't see it from the bathroom door. Locate the toilet in its own alcove or behind a wall or screen. When this is not possible, hang a round-faceted cut-glass crystal from the ceiling between the door and the toilet to help lift and circulate the Ch'i (see Crystals, page 45).

BATHROOMS, CONT'D.

Make all bathrooms beautiful! You can quickly lift the Ch'i with a fresh coat of paint, new towels, art objects, and plants.

INNER WORK—*This inner work is about the draining and cleansing forces in your life. Sit quietly for a few minutes and ask if you are being environmentally, emotionally, mentally, or spiritually drained in some way. If you are, it's time to lift this downward pull on your vitality. Don't let anything drain your Ch'i! Cleanse yourself of anyone or anything that is pulling you down, and close the drains, literally and figuratively!*

BEAMS

Overhead beams are a popular structural feature in Western architecture and are considered to add character. They can also add a sense of heaviness and danger over your head, especially when you sit or sleep

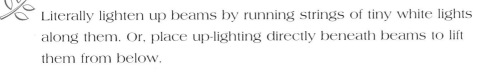
directly under them. The bigger, darker, and lower they are, the more you want to lighten them up.

 Paint or refinish beams to match the ceiling color. Or, paint them white or a light pastel color.

 Literally lighten up beams by running strings of tiny white lights along them. Or, place up-lighting directly beneath beams to lift them from below.

Symbolically break the beam's heaviness by hanging two objects at angles that suggest a drawbridge partially open (/ \ ). You can use two bamboo flutes, hung with the mouthpieces down to symbolize the Ch'i flowing up to lift the beam. Or hang things that imply a lifting and lightening of the beam, such as feathers and ribbons. Appropriate subject matter such as vines and birds can also be painted on beams to artistically lighten their presence.

 Hang beautiful handwoven textiles, prayer flags, floral swags, banners, mobiles, or any other *lightweight* items from the beam (see Flowers, page 66; and Wind Dancers, page 125).

BEAMS, CONT'D.

 When applicable, soften the hard line of a beam by rounding its sharp edges. Or add curves at each end of the beam to simulate an arch.

 Canopy your bed when there's a beam over it and you cannot move the bed to another location.

INNER WORK—*Beams symbolize burdens. Are you feeling overwhelmed or burdened by something in life? It's time to face what's weighing you down. Even if there is nothing you can do about the burden, you have complete power over your attitude toward it. Decide what you can to do to lift your spirits and bring some joy and levity into your life. Repeat Louise Hay's affirmation, "ALL IS WELL. EVERYTHING IS WORKING OUT FOR MY HIGHEST GOOD. OUT OF THIS SITUATION ONLY GOOD WILL COME. I AM SAFE!"*

Hang beautiful handwoven textiles, prayer flags, floral swags, banners, mobiles, or any other lightweight items from the beam.

BEDROOMS

Because our Western culture puts little importance on rest, our bedrooms are frequently not conducive to a good night's sleep. Ideally, our bedrooms are a perfect combination of cozy nest, rejuvenating oasis, and romantic hideaway—a sensual embrace where we go to completely recharge our batteries.

— ALL BEDROOMS

Locate bedrooms toward the back of the house, where the Ch'i is naturally more serene.

Dedicate your bedroom to its original role—the room for the BED. Locate possessions that require active Ch'i, such as exercise equipment and desks, in other rooms. Or, place "active" furniture and equipment as far from the bed as possible, screened or covered when not in use.

13

Choose your bed placement carefully. You know your bed is ideally located when you have a view of the door from the bed, without being directly in front of the door. This puts you in a peaceful "eddy" of the room, with a commanding view of the door. When architecture dictates that your bed is directly in front of the door, put a substantial footboard, trunk, table, or seat at the foot of the bed. When your bed has no direct view of the door, hang a small mirror to reflect the door from the bed. Your bed can be placed at a diagonal as long as you have a solid headboard or screen behind you. Windows can cause drafts and an unsafe feeling and should not be directly over the bed.

 Choose your colors carefully. The best bedroom colors are the skin colors found in all the races of people around the world. These include creamy beiges and browns, pinks, yellows, reds, and lavenders; as well as the deeper tones of chocolate, coral, raspberry, butter cream, burgundy, and aubergine. Pure white, black, gray, blue, and cool greens can be included but will make the bedroom chilly and less inviting if they dominate.

Serene, romantic, and sensual art belongs in the bedroom.

 Choose your art carefully. Serene, romantic, and sensual art belongs in the bedroom. Three-ring circuses and busy cityscapes do not. Hang only lightweight pieces over the bed.

 Choose your furniture carefully. Does it carry any "downer" memories, such as a death or divorce? Are there sharp corners or edges that could be dangerous to sleepy—or amorous—body parts? Ideally, all your bedroom furniture is extraordinarily comfortable and safe.

 The view from your bed influences your view of the world. It's what you see the first thing in the morning and last thing at night. Make it a good one! Shut, curtain, or screen bathroom or closet doors, and create a view with art, plants, and furniture that's especially pleasing.

 Many people see a television from their bed. Be sure it's housed in a cabinet with doors so that it can disappear between uses. TVs are watched more often when they are in plain view and

The view from your bed influences your view of the world.

BEDROOMS, CONT'D.

perpetually "staring" at their owners. Consider relocating the TV to another room.

Feng Shui rule of thumb: Hang one mirror at the most in the bedroom (see Mirrors, page 95). Mirrors activate Ch'i and can keep a bedroom "awake" all night long. The bigger the mirror is and the closer it is to the bed, the more likely it will disturb the peace. Treat large mirrored closet doors like windows. Curtain them so that you can open and close them as needed. Drape or screen other mirrors before retiring at night. Insomnia has been cured by this simple act.

Check under the bed to be sure it is free of clutter. The Ch'i of anything under the bed is affecting you every night!

INNER WORK— *You are worthy of having a truly sensual, comforting bedroom that feels fantastic every morning and every night, and you deserve to celebrate yourself with Ch'i-enhancing influences such as extra soft linens and extraordinary art. Celebrate your bedroom and affirm:*

Check under the bed to be sure it is free of clutter.

"IN THE SPIRIT OF CONSTANT RENEWAL, I EXPERIENCE COMPLETE REST AND REJUVENATION IN MY BEDROOM EVERY NIGHT."

— MASTER BEDROOMS

Make your master bedroom a sensual place, meaning a place where all your senses are celebrated. Add romantic music and sensuous fabrics, include scented oils and candles, drink something delicious in bed, and choose art and colors that visually wrap you in their warm embrace.

No matter how big your master bedroom is, make it cozy and romantic. Most people like to feel nestled into their bedrooms, completely secure and sheltered from the world. If your bedroom is large, create two or more cozy places to enjoy.

Move photographs of children and family to another location. Your romantic life will improve if photos of your kids and parents aren't staring at you in bed.

BEDROOMS, CONT'D.

Couples who share the same view from their bed also tend to share the same point of view in life. Make the view from your bed absolutely wonderful, with art or other features that *both partners* find very pleasing.

Make sure there's adequate space and attractive nightstands on *both* sides of the bed.

Be diligent about locating a television behind closed doors. In most cases, when TV viewing increases in the bedroom, lovemaking decreases.

INNER WORK—*Are the lines of communication open in your relationship? If not, it's time to clear the Ch'i by telling your partner what you are feeling and what would make you happy. Ask what your partner is feeling and what would make him or her happy. Having a heart-to-heart talk is often the quickest way to reawaken the romantic feelings that brought you together. Whatever the outcome, knowing the truth will set you free to grow, and to pursue the happiness you deserve.*

Photographs of parents and grandparents make children feel secure and "watched over" at night.

— CHILDREN'S BEDROOMS

Unlike the master bedroom, it's a good idea to have family photos in children's bedrooms. Photographs of parents and grandparents make children feel secure and "watched over" at night.

Many "hyperactive" children are sleeping in bedrooms with bright red sheets, and walls full of action figures. Calm their bedrooms by replacing bright reds, blues, and yellows with warm pastels and deep rich tones that wrap children in a cozy, tranquil embrace. Bring in serene or happy art that isn't flying, falling, driving, or running around the room.

Children are often very sensitive to mirrors. If your kids are not sleeping well, be sure to curtain, cover, or remove mirrors from their bedrooms.

 Pets living in children's bedrooms, such as hamsters, turtles, and fish, should be well taken care of. A neglected pet actually drains the vital Ch'i in a youngster's bedroom.

 When children share a bedroom, give each child a distinct place to call his or her own, such as a table, closet, or shelf. This keeps each child's Ch'i individually defined, and helps them learn to respect one another's space.

— SINGLE WOMEN'S BEDROOMS

These suggestions are for single women who want romance in their lives:

 Stuffed animals and dolls on the bed "whisper" to a new lover that the bed is already taken. Make room for romance by giving them a home somewhere else.

Put inviting nightstands and lamps on both sides of your bed.

Romantic spontaneity is hampered by a sea of pillows on the bed, so cull the pillow herd. Design a sensuous, unencumbered bed that you can fall into without a "single" care.

Change art portraying companionless figures, solitary flowers, and other "onesome" subjects to "twosome" art: two people, animals, flowers, or two of anything that inspires you.

Place pairs of items, such as candlesticks, vases, and books in the Love and Marriage area of your home and your bedroom (see Bagua Map, page 131).

Act as if you already have a partner! Put inviting nightstands and lamps on *both* sides of your bed.

Set the stage for receiving your new love by giving yourself the same loving care that you'd give a lover. Your loving relationship with yourself will strengthen your Ch'i and make you more attractive as a partner. Create a romantic atmosphere for yourself. Enjoy your own company, and find out what it's like to really love *you*.

BEDROOMS, CONT'D.

INNER WORK—*Make sure you believe that you deserve the perfect love partner, and that it's possible to experience the romance of your dreams. Align your inner beliefs and feelings so that you know you can attract and enjoy romantic happiness. Post affirmations around your house that affirm your certainty and excitement about your upcoming romance, such as "I ATTRACT WILDLY SATISFYING AND JOYFUL ROMANTIC RELATIONSHIPS INTO MY LIFE; or I AM A MAGNIFICENT PERSON, AND I NOW ATTRACT A HAPPY, HEALTHY, JOYFUL LOVER INTO MY LIFE." Along with your affirmations, make a detailed list of the qualities you want in your lover. Read your list daily, and change it as much as you like.*

— SINGLE MEN'S BEDROOMS

These suggestions are for men who want to attract romance into their lives:

 Is your bedroom a multipurpose room where you work out, watch TV, surf the Net, write proposals, and (supposedly) rest? Although this arrangement may be practical, it is not the slightest bit romantic. To attract a partner, make room for romance. Put your active equipment, TV, and computer in other rooms. If any of these items need to stay in your bedroom, screen or cover them when they're not in use. Let your bed command your bedroom, and keep your bed linens clean and welcoming.

 Check your art. Introduce artistic elements that suggest sensuality and serenity, and move "single guy" art such as cars, centerfolds, or basketball stars to another location.

INNER WORK—*Are you absolutely certain that you are ready for the perfect love partner to come into your life? Are you willing to change your life to include an intimate relationship? Align your inner beliefs and feelings so that you can trust and enjoy romantic happiness. Say affirmations such as "I ATTRACT A ROMANTIC PARTNER WHO MAKES MY LIFE BETTER AND MORE WONDERFUL IN EVERY WAY. IN LOVE, I AM FREE AND HAPPY." Along with your affirmations, make a detailed list of the qualities you want in your lover. Read it daily and change it as much as you like.*

— GUEST ROOMS

When you truly have the space for a guest room, don't "tourniquet" it off from the rest of the house. Make it beautiful and comfortable, leave the door open, and visit the room regularly, if only to water plants or open a window. Guard against it becoming a junk room that gets shoveled out just before guests arrive.

Don't limit your work needs or creative expression! If you need a place to work, make art, dance, or exercise, redesign the guest room. There are many ways you can incorporate a guest bed into your new design, including Murphy beds, hideabeds, and futons.

BLESSINGS

Blessings have been a part of life since the beginning of time. In Feng Shui, when you bless your home, you are blessing the dynamic "being who" houses and protects you every day and night. Bless and celebrate your home frequently with your thoughts and actions, and remember that no matter how many times blessings are performed, it is your personal Ch'i that gives them life. The quality of your inner life is directly reflected in your home. No amount of outer blessing will bring light into your home if you are unwilling to carry it within you. In essence, you are the blessing.

C

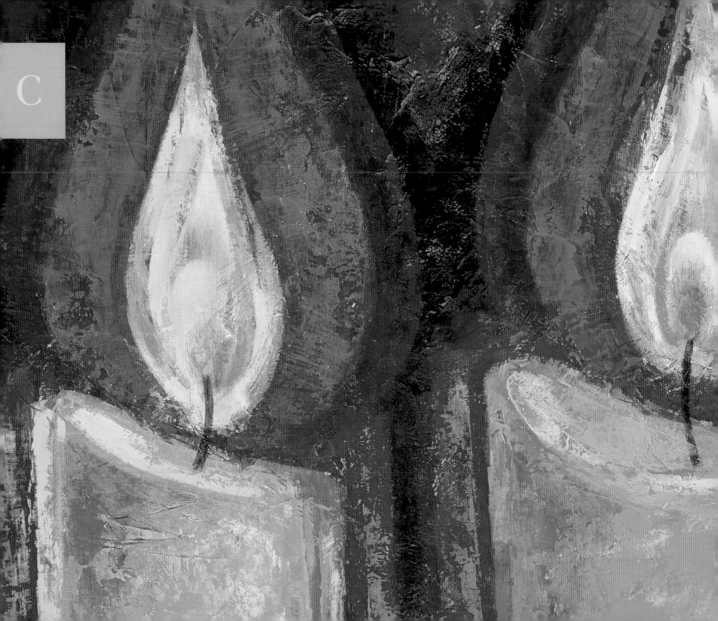

Candles enhance the Ch'i by bringing light, warmth, and color into your home.

CANDLES

Candles enhance the Ch'i by bringing light, warmth, and color into your home. With a variety of shapes and sizes available, they provide a fun, inexpensive way to experiment with new colors and scents. They are also instant "space shifters"; they can change a mundane environment into an enchanting one with the strike of a match. Candles can create an introspective atmosphere for meditation, a sensual mood for romance, or an environment of warmth and good cheer for your friends. The best candles are dripless, and either unscented or naturally scented.

CEILINGS

Our ceilings provide us with protection and safety. For most people, the ideal ceiling height is between eight and ten feet. Lower ceilings can feel heavy overhead, while higher ceilings can feel too open to protect us. If you have a room that's either hobbit- or giant-sized, there are ways you can balance the ceiling to feel just right for you.

Ceilings, cont'd.

— LOW CEILINGS

 One of your best "fix-its" in a room with a low ceiling is up-lighting. Make sure to use light fixtures and lamps that focus the light up toward the ceiling, not down toward the floor.

 Paint the ceiling white or a light pastel. This will lift the perceived height of the ceiling, especially when your up-lights are on.

 Use light and bright colors throughout the room. Furnishings that are scaled low also help lift the perceived height of the ceiling.

— HIGH CEILINGS

High ceilings require definition between "Heaven and Earth" to make the room comfortable.

Use crown molding, stenciling, or wallpaper borders to draw a horizontal line around the room anywhere from eight to ten feet above the floor. Once the line is drawn, you have the option of painting or wallpapering the walls differently above and below the line.

A line can also be suggested by hanging art pieces around the room at the same height. The eye will then "fill in the blanks." The tops of furniture, windows, or doors may already suggest a horizontal line that can be strengthened by hanging your art at the same height. Keep the branches of large plants below the line. Your objective is to balance the ceiling's vertical height with one subtle horizontal line around the room.

Once the line between Heaven and Earth has been established, you can hang items above it in the "Heavens," such as a chandelier suspended from the ceiling. Wind dancers (page 125) such as mobiles, banners, and textiles can also be used. Be sure to hang only lightweight items directly over furniture.

CEILINGS, CONT'D.

Canopy beds are great in bedrooms with high ceilings. Canopied fabrics can also be used to create intimate nooks, places for conversation, and reading areas.

Dark, rich tones in furnishings and ceiling color help to give weight and substance to rooms with high ceilings.

CEILING FANS

Ceiling fans are a necessity in some climates. They dissipate heat and create a refreshing breeze in an otherwise stifling environment, yet they can appear dangerous if not positioned correctly in a room.

Ceiling fans that are situated directly over beds, desks, or dining tables can disturb relaxation and concentration, so be sure to install them away from furniture you often sit on.

In general, the higher the fans are, the better. When low, they can feel dangerous to anyone passing underneath. The same ominous feeling occurs when fans dominate rooms in size, color, or ornamentation. Fans work best when they blend into the background and are of simple design.

CHAIRS

Because comfort is so important in Feng Shui, ergonomics (the study of the human body's physiostructural needs) plays an important role. Chairs can either invite relaxation or cause stress and discomfort, negatively affecting body alignment and peace of mind. Make sure the chairs you choose—whether for dining, lounging, or working—are comfortable.

Your body knows! Always sit in a chair before buying it. Chairs should fit your body and be very comfortable. Most wooden, plastic, and metal chairs need to be padded or cushioned.

CHAIRS, CONT'D.

Insist on a comfortable work chair. If your company won't supply it for you, buy one for yourself. You are worth it! (See Offices, page 99.)

INNER WORK—*Chairs represent kindness. A classic act of kindness is to offer a person a comfortable place to sit. Do you do this for yourself? Are you kind enough to yourself to make your own comfort and support a priority? Think of something kind you can do for yourself each day, and do it. Say affirmations such as "KINDNESS, COMFORT, AND SUPPORT SURROUND ME ALL THE TIME. I ATTRACT HAPPY, SUPPORTIVE PEOPLE INTO MY LIFE, TODAY AND ALWAYS."*

CHAOS

Chaos is part of the cycle of life. Because we cannot live without creating chaos on a regular basis, it's important to understand the two kinds of chaos.

Active chaos has to occur to birth anything.

— ACTIVE CHAOS

This is the kind of chaos we see spinning around a chef as he prepares a feast, or around a painter as she creates a masterpiece. Even in the presence of dirty pans or spilled paints, we are drawn to their "mess" like bees to honey. The Ch'i hums and dances as a new creation is being born. Our excitement and curiosity are piqued as we experience what the creator is bringing to life. Active chaos has to occur to birth anything—from a fine meal, to a new garden or a lovely work of art. The key to keeping chaos active is to clean up the mess and reorganize our materials between creative bursts. Then, when the next wave of creativity hits, we are ready to dive in.

— PASSIVE CHAOS

A mess left for long becomes passive chaos. It's the kitchen that wasn't cleaned up after the feast, or it's the studio where paints were left open to dry in their tubes. Passive chaos grows in unattended drawers, corners, and basements. It's what many of us see when we drive into our garages or open our closet doors. We know it's passive chaos when it annoys, confuses, or stops us. There's no lively Ch'i there, just a big *old* mess. Passive chaos is draining and actually pushes us away, making it very challenging to face the jumble and return it to order. The last thing we want to do is clean it up, and the longer it sits there, the more draining it gets.

As you plow through passive chaos, ask yourself the following questions about the items you find. This will help you get organized.

Seven "Clear the Way" Questions

1. Do I love it?
2. Do I need it?
3. Does it support who I am *now* in my life?
4. Does it act as an environmental affirmation for me?
5. What positive and/or negative thoughts, memories, or emotions do I associate with it?
6. Does it need to be fixed or repaired, and am I willing to do so now?
7. If it's time to let it go, am I going to sell, lend, or give it away, and when?

As you bravely face passive chaos in your own home, know that you are inviting transformation to occur. In attending to the old, you are clearing the way for many new positive opportunities to flow into your life.

INNER WORK—*Passive chaos symbolizes old thoughts and patterns that "mess up" the quality of your life. Take an inner inventory. Do you have attitudes and feelings that keep you from enjoying life? Are you chronically annoyed, confused, or impeded from moving forward? If so, decide how you can clean out those pockets of passive chaos and renew your own inner environment. Affirm that "I CLEAR AND CLEAN MY BODY, HEART, AND SOUL, KNOWING THAT THE MORE I LET GO OF THE OLD, THE MORE I ATTRACT NEW, INSPIRING, ENJOYABLE PEOPLE, PLACES, AND THINGS INTO MY LIFE. I TRUST THAT ALL OF MY NEEDS ARE MET AS THEY ARISE ALL THE TIME."*

"The more I let go of the old, the more I attract the new."

CH'I

Ch'i means "vital energy." Everything is alive with Ch'i, connected by Ch'i, and the Ch'i in everything is always changing. Seeing the world as a dynamic, ever-changing "Sea of Ch'i" helps us understand why Feng Shui promotes the building and enhancing of vital Ch'i flow in our homes. We do this by arranging our furniture and possessions in specific ways, living with what we love, and adopting designs that promote safety and comfort. We also simplify and thoroughly organize our environment to encourage clarity and creative self-expression. We know we've struck the ideal Ch'i chord in our homes when we are experiencing happy, healthy, and prosperous lives.

INNER WORK—*How do you cultivate your own inner Ch'i? Besides sleeping and eating, how do you rejuvenate yourself on a daily basis? Ch'i is cultivated in many ways, including bathing, exercising, practicing Tai Ch'i or yoga, reading, journaling, meditating, gardening, dancing, singing, making love, playing music, going to the theater, laughing, creating and enjoying art, giving and receiving bodywork, cooking, caring for*

36

pets, and being out in nature. Add your favorite ways to the list, and make it a top priority to cultivate your personal Ch'i every day.

CH'I ENHANCERS

Each Ch'i enhancer is described under its own heading throughout this book. Please keep in mind that the best Ch'i enhancers are the ones you love. Always be guided by your personal tastes in:

1. animals
2. art
3. colors
4. crystals
5. flowers
6. lighting
7. plants
8. mirrors
9. nature objects
10. sound makers
11. water features
12. wind dancers

CLEANSING

Cleaning our homes removes not only dirt and clutter, but also stagnant, unhealthy energy. We all know what a difference living in a clean house makes to our sense of well-being. Still, there are times when a room looks clean but doesn't feel clean. There's a stale, sticky, or spooky feeling that seems to cling to the room. Many people feel this when they move into homes that were previously occupied and are sensitive enough to feel the unsettling energy of a former owner's tragedy or unhappiness. In these cases, it's important to "deep-clean" the space in question.

 When moving into a home that has previously been occupied, be sure to have the carpets cleaned and the walls painted. In most cases, this neutralizes the energy of the people who lived there before you and puts your personal signature on your "new" home.

 Spray a cleansing mist along the baseboards and into all the corners to revitalize a space. Cleansing mists contain citrus oil and can be purchased where health food and aromatherapy products are sold. Or make your own by adding a couple of drops of orange or lemon essential oils to an atomizer filled with water.

Spray a cleansing mist along the baseboards and into all the corners to revitalize a space.

Most Feng Shui practitioners are trained to energetically cleanse homes. In extreme cases, when ghosts or poltergeists are suspected, you will need the expertise of someone who specializes in exorcism. In most cases, however, you can deep-clean a space quite well on your own.

Be sure to bless your home after a cleansing (see Blessings, page 24).

INNER WORK—*We all need a good emotional and spiritual cleansing from time to time. Don't allow your inner environment to become dark and spooky. Make sure you cleanse and cultivate your inner Ch'i (page 36) on a daily basis. And, at least once a year, refresh yourself by changing the scenery. Vacations, health retreats, and vision quests cleanse and enlighten your body, mind, and spirit.*

CLOSETS, DRAWERS, AND CABINETS

Closets, drawers, and cabinets are often the clutter hideaways and stagnant backwaters of a home, negatively affecting the flow of Ch'i throughout. The house may look orderly until you open a closet or drawer, and then all clutter breaks loose. Since there's no place to hide in Feng Shui, the organization and pleasing arrangement of things in these areas becomes as important as the organization and arrangement of your living room.

Please don't be overwhelmed; just take it one spot at a time. If it's a jumble in there, use the "Clear the Way" questions on page 34 to help you simplify and organize. Keep the items only if your answers are positive! If not, let them go, knowing the Ch'i in your entire home—and your life—will benefit.

INNER WORK—*Each item in a closet, drawer, or cabinet has a tale to tell about why it's still in your possession. Contemplate what each item is "saying" to you. Is it scolding you for gaining weight or being clumsy? Is it broken or torn? Is it something you never really liked anyway? Listen and learn from the things that "bring you down," and once you've heard what they have to say, let them go. Step fully into the present, your place of power, and let go of anything that doesn't have nice things to say. In so doing, your self-esteem will soar.*

COLLECTIONS

In our materially abundant culture, it's easy to collect items of interest. Some collections such as crystal, jewelry, and antiques involve making an investment with every new piece, while other collections are meaningful because of the memories they hold. Whatever you collect, make sure you are managing it, and not vice versa.

Determine if you are still interested in your collection. People often lose interest in the items they've collected, in the same way that children outgrow certain kinds of toys. Let go of collections that no longer interest you to make plenty of room to pursue your new interests.

Decide if there are pieces that no longer belong there. As your collection evolves, make room for the new by sorting out the ones that no longer fit.

Enjoy your collections. This keeps the house nourished with the Ch'i that comes from loving what you live with. You may have room to display only part of a collection at any given time. Revolving your collection renews it as you circulate pieces from storage to display and back again.

Like art, collections can be lent to friends, the local library, museums, hospitals, schools, or galleries so others can enjoy them. When you are ready to let go of a collection permanently, do so in a way that honors the time and work you put into it. This will give you a sense of completion and free you to enjoy your new interests.

INNER WORK—*As you enjoy your worldly collections, make sure to build your inner collections as well. By their very nature, your collections of things come and go, while your store of inner wisdom, self-esteem, and inspiration is timeless.*

COLORS

Because color is a very personal and powerful tool for enhancing the Ch'i in your home, make sure to surround yourself with the colors that feed and nurture you. New colors can be easily introduced via flowers, candles, fabrics, and other decor. However, removing or replacing paint,

Colors add a powerful healing quality to your home.

carpet, and upholstery in your home is usually a big job. You can't just throw them off at the end of the day like a bright red shirt or yellow dress. You will live, eat, and sleep with your color choices for a while.

This isn't to suggest that you should be timid with color, just smart. Experiment with color before ordering enough to fill a room. For instance, before buying a bright blue couch, lay out bright blue paper or fabric where the couch will be, and live with it for a week or so. Are you still as in love with the color on the eighth day as you were on the first? If certain wall colors look good in a magazine, try painting a section of your wall that color, put your furniture or artwork against it, and live with it for a few days. You may find that you'd like it deeper, richer, paler, or not at all. If you live with other people, make sure they like the colors you're choosing. Take your time. When chosen well, colors add a powerful healing quality to your home.

When working with the Bagua Map (page 131), use the color associations that you find appealing. Don't feel pressured to use black to enhance your Career area, or red to bolster your Fame and Reputation area unless you like these colors. *Any color enhances the Ch'i if it inspires you each time you see it.*

COLORS, CONT'D.

INNER WORK—*Ask, "What color is my essence?" There's a color that is "you," which deeply nurtures and energizes you every time you see it. Introduce your soul essence color into your environment in just the perfect way—perhaps in the brilliant glaze of a ceramic bowl or the soft folds of a throw across your bed. Because your soul color resonates so personally with you, it is especially revitalizing for you to have it in your home. When you need some extra energy, gaze at your color and fill yourself up with it, or visualize it anywhere, anytime, to achieve the same healing results.*

Ask those you live with what color their soul or essence is. The answer can strengthen relationships with spouses, friends, and children. In one case, a couple determined that he was "golden yellow" while she was "turquoise green," so they added a pillow in each color to their couch to symbolize their togetherness.

CREATIVE EXPRESSION

Expressing yourself creatively is one of the most powerful ways to enhance the vitality of the Ch'i flowing through your home. Your creativity activates joy, enthusiasm, and participation in life. Your creative expression may include cooking, arranging flowers, playing music, singing, dancing, writing, building, planting, and artistic pursuits. Organize your environment to unleash your creativity, and enjoy being an inspiration to yourself and others.

INNER WORK—*Assess your creative expression. If you feel creatively blocked, what happened to shut down your creative juices? Do you make room in your life to be creative, or are you just too "busy"? Being creative is as vital to the health of your spirit as vitamin C is to the health of your body. It's your inner participation in the creative process that feeds your spirit. Begin today to nurture yourself in this way by doing something that will nurture your creativity. Decide which avenue of expression makes your heart sing, and give it to yourself as a gift!*

CRYSTALS

Round, faceted cut-glass crystals are used in Feng Shui to balance and moderate extremes in Ch'i flow. Crystals are considered transcendental "cures," meaning that they carry the strength of your intention to balance Ch'i that's moving too quickly or slowly through your home.

CRYSTALS, CONT'D.

Their small size makes them easy to use where there is no room for any other enhancement. Crystals are available at most gift shops, and range in size from 10 to 75 millimeters (mm), with 25 mm (one inch) being the most popular size for Feng Shui purposes.

 To slow down the "raging river" of Ch'i that flows down a long hallway, suspend crystals a few inches from the ceiling every ten feet or so down the hall, or install a light fixture made with faceted crystals.

 When there is a sharp corner protruding into a room, hang a crystal from the ceiling an inch or two away from the corner to modify the "cutting Ch'i."

 Hang a crystal above the bottom step of a staircase that faces the front door. This keeps the Ch'i from being swept out of the house too quickly.

Suspend a crystal in front of a small window that does not seem to bring enough light into the room.

❧ Hang a crystal in front of a large window, especially one with a commanding view. The larger the window, the larger the crystal. Or, you can hang several 25mm crystals in a large window.

PLEASE NOTE: Hanging crystals directly in windows that receive bright sun has caused fires. If the window you are working with gets a lot of sun, hang the crystal at a safe distance and height, or choose another enhancement.

❧ When a door and a window (or another door) are located directly across from each other, hang a crystal midway between them.

❧ If you can see the toilet from the bathroom door, hang a crystal midway between the door and toilet.

❧ Suspend a crystal in front of a small window that does not seem to bring enough light into the room.

CRYSTALS, CONT'D.

 Hang a crystal in the center of a house (or any room) that feels stagnant or in need of cleansing. This works best when it's the only crystal in the house or room. If you want to put crystals in other places, remove the one in the center.

 Be sure to clean your crystals weekly to keep them shiny and bright.

Our dining rooms become our oases where we nourish and renew our bodies, hearts, and spirits.

DINING ROOMS

In many homes, the dining room table and chairs sit empty most of the time, brought to life only during parties or holidays. Some homes don't have a dining room per se, but a nook or area within a larger room in which to dine. Whether it's a place or a room, chances are that it's not often used. Our cultural tendency is to rush through most of our meals perched at the kitchen counter, standing over the sink, or sitting in front of the television. The fine art of dining has been relegated to the occasional special event.

When we reclaim the deeply nourishing experience of enjoying our meals in a pleasant and serene dining environment, we become more aware of the Ch'i qualities in our food. Our heightened awareness tunes us into the essential vitality that is being passed to us in every meal. We also receive the gift of connecting with ourselves, as well as with others who may be breaking bread with us, partaking of both food for the body and food for thought. Our dining rooms become our oases where, with gratitude, we nourish and renew our bodies, hearts, and spirits.

DINING ROOMS, CONT'D.

 Comfort is inherent in the positive flow of Ch'i. So, just like in every other room, make sure your dining room furniture is very comfortable. Sit in your dining room chairs, and notice whether or not your body relaxes. If not, pad the chairs or replace them.

 Even when your chairs are comfortable, are they safe? Check for protruding legs that could snag a toe, or sharp detailing that could tear clothing. Repair or replace chairs that are rickety or torn.

 How do the table and chairs interact? Are they too high or low to work well together? This can happen even when the dining table and chairs were made as a set. Pad, alter, or replace ill-fitting furniture as needed. And, be sure you can easily scoot your chair under the table without hitting supports or the base of the table.

 If the table has sharp edges or corners, as many glass tables do, soften them with cloths or table runners. Positioning your table diagonally in the room may also reduce the danger.

Choose a dining table that's an appropriate size for daily use.

Make sure your dining area is defined enough to have its own identity. Screens, plants, lighting, area rugs, and furniture placement can help define a space that encourages reflection, digestion, and intimate conversation.

Choose art that relaxes and inspires you. Mirrors, especially when large, can overactivate a room meant to be tranquil.

Choose a dining table that's an appropriate size for daily use. Two people aren't drawn to eat at a table big enough for eight. In large homes, there may be a formal dining room furnished for entertaining, which is fine if there is another dedicated dining area for daily use. To make a large table feel more intimate, drape and set it at one end, and use the rest to display things you love, such as flowers, candles, and collectibles.

DOORS

In Feng Shui, your front door (see Front Entrances, page 68) is considered the primary Mouth of Ch'i. All other doors are smaller "mouths" through which the breath of Ch'i, like fresh air, meanders through the rooms of your house.

When building a home or addition, plan on doing one of two things. Either locate your doors so that they are *not* directly across from other doors or large windows (see Windows, page 125); or plan to leave enough room to be able to place a piece of furniture, a planter, an island, or a screen between them. This is to encourage Ch'i to meander through a room like a refreshing breeze rather than moving too quickly through the room

When you are living in a home that has doors lined up directly across from other doors or large windows, and you cannot put something substantial in between them, hang a crystal (see Crystals, page 45) from the ceiling midway between them to help circulate the Ch'i streaming through the room.

Check all the doors in your home to make sure they open fully and easily. Relocate anything stored behind a door that blocks its full range of motion.

 Repair all doors that are sticky, loose, or in need of new hardware or paint.

 Hang attractive items such as mirrors, paintings, or photographs directly across from doors in confined spaces such as hallways and foyers.

The area around any door should be well lit. Make sure lights or light switches are conveniently located near all your doors, including those in halls, basements, and attics.

INNER WORK—*Doors symbolize our ability to make clear, intelligent decisions in life. Each day we have multiple opportunities to stand at the threshold of an experience and make a decision—yes or no. How would*

Hang attractive items in confined spaces such as hallways and foyers.

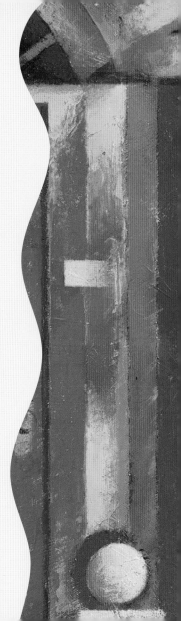

Wisdom and clarity come from knowing your purpose in life.

DOORS, CONT'D.

you rate your ability to clearly and easily make decisions? Do you frequently say yes, whether or not the experience is good for you? Do you often say no, slamming the door on ripe possibilities? Or, do you remain indecisive until the door of opportunity has closed? Ideally, your ability to say yes or no has full range of motion, based on your own inner wisdom and clarity.

Wisdom and clarity come from knowing your purpose in life. Arnold Patent, author of You Can Have It All, suggests that you ask: "What is my purpose for living?" or "What is my unique role in the Universe?" The simpler your answer, the more powerful it will be. Define your purpose in life, and watch your ability to choose which doors in life to walk through become crystal clear.

ELECTRICAL EQUIPMENT

Many practitioners of Feng Shui consider electrical equipment to be enhancers of Ch'i, and they certainly can be when properly used and well taken care of. Most of us have electrical appliances in every room, so we need to be conscious of the effect these "beings" have on our lives. A television can be a fabulous source of information and entertainment, but it can also devour family interaction, romantic interludes, and peaceful silence. Electrical equipment makes a wonderful servant or a very unfortunate master. Feng Shui addresses how to keep these "servants" in their rightful place so they add only richness, enjoyment, and vital Ch'i to our lives.

One of the best ways you can live in harmony with electrical equipment is to give each piece a home. House them in appliance garages, armoires, built-in cabinets, or drawers when not in use. Or cover equipment with fitted cloths or fabric that suit the decor of the room. Our credo for balance is "Out of sight, out of mind." Equipment behind closed doors or beneath an attractive cover is more in harmony with the natural rhythms of life and less in command of every room in the house.

The electromagnetic field (EMF) of our electrical and battery-powered equipment is a concern we also need to address. An EMF tester shows the "field of influence" around all electrical kitchen, bathroom, office, and entertainment equipment and appliances. You'll probably be surprised at how much EMF you receive each day, and you may choose to sit or stand farther away from your electrical things. Life-giving Ch'i-enhancers such as plants, flowers, and water features help to balance the EMF in your home.

ENVIRONMENTAL AFFIRMATIONS

In an ideal world, your entire home is one big Environmental Affirmation. You are surrounded by objects and architecture that lift your spirits and please your senses, have wonderful feelings and memories associated with them, and continually affirm your harmony and balance

In an ideal world, your entire home is one big Environmental Affirmation.

in life. When so benevolently surrounded, your environment acts like a giant cornucopia of positive Ch'i, and you are constantly nourished and strengthened by your material world.

To reach this goal, start by looking at the things and the architecture you live with. Decide what you love and what you don't. If you don't love much about your current home, don't be discouraged! You can improve the situation immediately by putting one object you do like in each room. You can use any of the Ch'i Enhancers listed on page 37 to make instant improvements. This begins the process of enhancing the Ch'i flow and attracting the things that uplift you. Begin where you can, and watch your world change for the better.

When you live with other people who have different tastes, you won't necessarily have the luxury of living with only those things you love. Some room designs will have to be based on compromise. Ideally, a man has the blessing of the rest of the household before he hangs his deer trophies in the family room; a woman knows if her husband will live happily with ribbons and lace before filling the bedroom with them; roommates ask each other before hanging their poster art collection on the kitchen walls. The inevitable need to compromise in shared spaces emphasizes the requirement for people to have their own private area. Let each person in a household claim a niche, room, or whole area, and design it to completely affirm who they are and what they love.

ENVIRONMENTAL AFFIRMATIONS, CONT'D.

INNER WORK—Ask yourself, "Am I creating an affirming inner environment of positive thoughts and feelings? Or is my inner atmosphere crowded with old, ways of thinking and feeling?" Replace negative thoughts and emotions with positive ones. As your inner world becomes more affirming, your outer world will reflect your focus. Say affirmations such as: "I LIVE IN AN ENVIRONMENT OF POSITIVE PEOPLE AND EXPERIENCES. I AM LOVING AND KIND IN ALL MY THOUGHTS, WORDS, AND ACTIONS. EVERY MOMENT OF MY LIFE IS BEAUTIFUL AND HARMONIOUS."

Create an environment thoughts and filled with positive and feelings.

F

The ideal family room serves multiple functions.

FAMILY ROOMS

Family rooms, or great rooms, tend to be multi-use rooms and need to be well thought out and organized according to everyone's needs. A small child needs a place to play with toys. An older child needs a place to do homework and use a computer. Adults and children alike need a place to socialize, watch television, listen to music, romp around, and eat the casual meal. The ideal family room functions as a place for all these activities.

Include adequate storage, such as chests, trunks, drawers, and cabinets for each family member. You'll stay more organized when the things used in family rooms are also stored there—easy in, easy out.

Put electrical equipment behind closed doors. Choose furniture that allows you to store televisions and stereos out of sight.

Choose bright, happy art and colors for your family room.

FAMILY ROOMS, CONT'D.

 When you have a computer in the family room, integrate it fully into the overall design of the room. (See Offices, page 99.)

 Choose no-nonsense tables with rounded corners that are made from materials that can be bumped, scratched, and spilled on without damage.

 Use easy-care floor coverings. This is no place for a priceless white rug!

 Choose bright, happy art and colors. Collections of family photos, children's art, travel posters, whimsical toys and games, or anything that's playful and fun belongs here.

 Include very comfy casual sofas and chairs. The Ch'i of family happiness flows best when the family room is as deliciously relaxing and indestructible as possible.

Fireplaces are archetypal symbols of comfort and safety.

FIREPLACES

A place of fire, be it hearth, wood stove, pellet burner, or gas fireplace, can be one of the most welcoming spots in a home. Fireplaces are archetypal symbols of comfort and safety, where people gather for warmth, conversation, and good cheer.

If your fireplace commands the room, you can balance it by placing objects representing the Water element nearby. These include mirrors; paintings of oceans, lakes, streams, and rivers; free-form art that suggests water; water features; black objects; and crystal and glass items.

Even when not in use, the fireplace should remain pleasing. Arrange fresh logs in preparation for the next fire; and place plants, flowers, or other attractive items in front of it to add interest and beauty to the room.

When not used for fires, consider making the fireplace a display "grotto." Use your imagination, and arrange beautiful objects such as candles, statues, and flowers inside the fireplace.

FLOWERS

Flowers are one of the easiest ways to uplift the Ch'i in our homes. They provide us with a sampling of nature's wonder and beauty and help us stay connected with the natural world.

Just as flowers can easily lift the Ch'i, they can also deplete it if not properly cared for. Keep your living flowers looking fresh. Once they begin to decline, groom or replace them with new ones. Only beautiful, vibrant flowers enhance and enliven the Ch'i!

Silk and plastic flowers are an alternative to fresh ones.

 Dried flowers, including wreaths and swags, are an alternative to fresh flowers. Many people think they last for years, but In most cases, dried flowers need to be replaced every three or four months. The smaller and more delicate they are, the sooner they break and fade, becoming Ch'i depleters rather than Ch'i enhancers. Dust them weekly with a hair dryer, and replace them when they lose their luster.

 Potpourri, normally made of dried flowers, needs to be replaced as soon as it loses its scent, which can be as often as once a week. Choose potpourri that's been naturally scented with essential oils, or make your own by mixing "fresh" dried petals and leaves with your favorite natural scents.

Silk and plastic flowers are another alternative to fresh flowers. These have a longer lifespan than fresh or dried ones and will usually maintain their vitality for about a year. Keep them clean and dust-free, and replace them as soon as they begin to fade.

FRONT ENTRANCES

The area leading up to your front door, the threshold itself, and the area immediately inside the home, are all part of your front entrance. This is the place of first impressions, and the primary place where vital Ch'i enters your home. Ideally, your front entrance is "entrancing," symbolizing your desire to welcome guests. Roll out the welcome mat and make your front entrance fabulous. In so doing, you'll attract an abundance of nourishing Ch'i into your home.

— OUTDOORS

 Install an outdoor water feature near your front entrance to symbolize your desire to receive wealth and prosperity in all forms. Choose one that suits your entrance area—anything from a huge fountain to a small birdbath. If your fountain is directional, make sure it's directed *toward* the house. Whether you choose a flowing fountain or a vessel of still water, keep it very clean and in good repair.

Make the landscaping around your front entrance especially appealing.

 Make the landscaping around your front entrance especially inviting. Design a wide, welcoming path to your front door that is distinct and separate from the driveway. Let it meander so that people have a chance to slow down and enjoy your special touches before reaching your door. Place seating near the front door to suggest comfort and relaxation. Embellish it with flowers, wind chimes, and other beautiful appointments. Even in the most humble or confined areas, a friendly sign or seasonal wreath on the door carries welcoming Ch'i.

 Always keep the front path (and all paths) in good repair; and clear of overgrown plants, toys, hoses, pet bowls, and any other potential hazard.

Be sure your entire front entrance area is well lit, with attractive outdoor lighting. This assures comfort and safety, and also illuminates your beautiful entrance features at night.

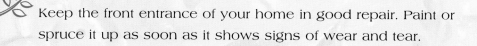

FRONT ENTRANCES, CONT'D.

Keep the front entrance of your home in good repair. Paint or spruce it up as soon as it shows signs of wear and tear.

In Feng Shui, the color red is often suggested to attract celebration, prosperity, and joy into the house. Many people paint their front doors an appealing shade of red, while others plant red flowers or place red objects near their front doors.

— *INDOORS*

Traditionally in Feng Shui, the best painting in the household is displayed by the front door. This is to honor everyone who enters your home. When you have the space, set up a welcoming arrangement that may include a painting, and a table appointed with items such as a vase of fresh flowers or an interior fountain. When your entry area is small, hang an attractive mirror, or art that has depth to open up the space. Create a token place of welcome even when there's no official foyer. Do whatever you can to present your guests—and yourself—with a warm and welcoming first impression.

Consider making your home a "shoeless" house. Design a place near the front door to store shoes. You might even want to provide socks or slippers for guests. This helps keep your home clean, and symbolizes leaving your worldly cares and concerns at the door.

As with the outdoor entrance area, keep the indoor path clear of migrating possessions such as toys, sports equipment, recyclables, and mail.

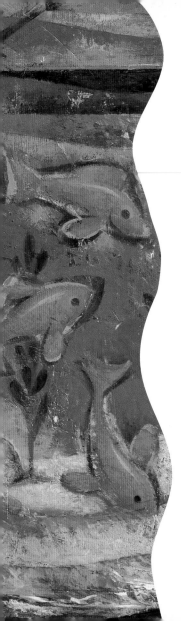

INNER WORK—*Do you feel that you are open to receiving all the goodness life holds for you? Are your inner doors open to welcoming happy, healthy relationships with yourself, your family, neighbors, co-workers, and friends? Affirm that only safe, loving people and experiences are attracted to your threshold. Breathe deeply and say, "WITH JOY AND GRATITUDE, I WELCOME AN ABUNDANCE OF POSITIVE PEOPLE AND EXPERIENCES INTO MY LIFE, NOW AND ALWAYS."*

"With joy and gratitude, I welcome abundance into my life."

GARAGES

Garages are specifically designed to house our transportation, and like stables built for horses and carriages, they were originally located behind the home. Economics and convenience now inspire builders to attach garages to the main house like an additional room, which poses some interesting Feng Shui challenges.

 When building a home, keep your garage *detached* from your main living quarters. This assures good air quality and a more peaceful flow of Ch'i throughout your home.

 Whether attached or detached, don't build a room directly over the garage. If you must, make it an "active" room, such as an office, studio, or playroom, *not* a bedroom other than a guest room. Fumes and the movement below do not promote relaxation, and can give the room an unsettled, restless feeling.

 If the garage is attached to your home, leave the garage door open for a few minutes after driving in, so that the fumes from the car don't get pulled into the house.

Avoid the tendency to let the garage become a chaotic storeroom. Make your garage a place you enjoy seeing every day. Leave plenty of room to drive in and out without worrying about hitting toys, equipment, or piles of laundry. Install shelves and cabinets for storage; and design attractive areas for working with plants, crafts, or engines. Make sure all trash and recycling containers are attractive, clean, and easy to access.

Your garage is often the last room you see when you leave and the first room you see when you return. Along with organizing it, give it personality and flair. Make it a "real room" by painting it your favorite color, hanging art, carpeting or painting the floor, and installing pleasant lighting that switches on when you drive in. You might even decide to turn the entire garage into an art studio, family room, or office.

GARDENS

Your garden is your personal passport into nature. It keeps you connected to the natural rhythms of life, while replenishing and sustaining

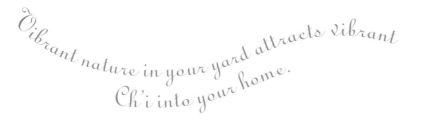

the Ch'i that meanders through your home. Walk by a house without land-scaping and you understand what a difference it makes. Whether your home has a green lawn with trees or an extensive flower and vegetable garden, keep it healthy and beautiful. Vibrant nature
in your yard attracts vibrant Ch'i into your home.

When applicable, use gardens and landscaping to complete the shape of your home (see the Bagua Map, page 131). If the overall shape of your home is not a whole square or rectangle, complete the shape by filling it in with any pleasing combination of trees, flower beds, garden sculptures, large rocks, decks, patios, fencing, lighting, specialty gardens, and water features. The "missing" area becomes a beautiful outdoor area, adding to the charm of your home.

Consider adding a still or flowing water feature to your front yard (see Front Entrances, page 68).

Create a natural embrace around the sides and back of your property with evergreen shrubs and trees, vines, fencing, or berms. Pay special

Gardens, cont'd.

attention to privatizing areas that are in view of neighbors' windows and doors. While your front yard is openly inviting, your side and back areas are your private retreat. Include pathways, tables, and seating in your outdoor garden design. As you enhance the embrace of nature around you, wildlife finds sanctuary in your yard, and you and your family can enjoy a private oasis.

 Make sure you have an attractive view from every window and door. Be nourished by a lovely view each time you look out of your home. Camouflage or screen unsightly views with plants, awnings, arbors, and hanging gardens. An inspirational place to rest the eye is a gift you give yourself every day.

When possible, set aside a place for a compost heap. It's very grounding and rejuvenating to make dirt. Louise Hay, author of *You Can Heal Your Life*, says, "*Just make good dirt, and God will do the rest.*" Composting allows you to participate in the natural cycle of life on a daily basis. Old carrot tops, fruit peelings, and coffee grounds become new soil. And, your garden benefits greatly from the rich compost you make.

Think about including a nature sanctuary in your garden design. These sanctuaries are not pruned, planted, or mowed. Instead, plants shape themselves, wildflowers flourish, and leaves decompose where they fall. As habitats for local flora and fauna, these wild areas build pure, natural Ch'i and provide privacy around your home.

INNER WORK—*This is a perfect time to plant your own inner garden. What aspects of your life would you like to see blossom? What dreams do you need to plant in fertile soil? Do you need to weed or dig out anything that's stifling your growth? Take a few minutes to contemplate your inner garden. See yourself planting the seeds and plants that represent the things that are important to you. Then, tend to your inner garden. Water and nurture it with intention and purpose, and enjoy the fruits of your inner work.*

HALLWAYS

In many homes, hallways lead from one part of the house to another. Unfortunately, they are often treated as "non-rooms" and remain dark and

Warm, friendly lighting in a hallway is a must.

HALLWAYS, CONT'D.

plain. The longer, thinner, and darker that hallways are, the more quickly we tend to hurry through them. Ideally, we want to be pleasantly drawn to slow down and enjoy a hallway's special touches.

Treat your hallway like a room with special qualities. It's perfectly shaped to be a gallery for displaying paintings, photographs, and posters, especially those with depth that "widen" the hall. Mirrors are also fine, as long as they aren't hung at the *end* of a long hallway, where they double the perceived length. Wider hallways can also be punctuated and given interest with furniture, bookshelves, carpets, and plants.

Warm, friendly lighting in a hallway is a must. Track lighting, crystal ceiling fixtures, wall sconces, and lamps assure safety and add beauty to hallways. The use of crystals in hallways is discussed on page 46, and the treatment of hallway doors is explored on page 55.

Choose a light pastel or vibrant color for your hallway's walls to give it a wider, brighter appearance.

HISTORY OF FENG SHUI

Feng Shui, meaning "Wind and Water," has been practiced for over 3,000 years in China. Students spent many years cultivating their Ch'i and acquiring the observational skills and inner wisdom necessary to practice Feng Shui. As practitioners, their work involved locating building sites imbued with the Ch'i, or vital energy, that would protect and nurture people and their interests. To find such auspicious locations, they walked the land, tasted the soil, looked for the telltale patterns made by wind and water, and watched for omens. Every physical feature and condition helped them decipher the Ch'i. Good omens, such as healthy plants, fertile soil, clear meandering streams, game animals, and songbirds, were signs that the Ch'i was "human friendly."

Feng Shui practitioners favored locations between the "foot and back of the dragon," or above a source of water such as a lake or stream, and below the tops of hills or mountains. These "belly of the dragon" areas were nestled between the extremes of wind and water, where the Ch'i embraced inhabitants and supported them in living safe, prosperous, and happy lives.

Feng Shui practitioners also guided the building process to assure that the Ch'i was not disturbed. This was taken very seriously. Buildings were "jewels," meticulously placed in their ideal settings upon the land. Rocks and trees used for building were blessed and carefully placed so that their Ch'i remained strong. When the building was complete, the practitioner blessed the house to ensure the family's prosperity, longevity, and happiness.

Feng Shui is as relevant in our Western world today as it was thousands of years ago in China. In our more material, less natural Western culture, we still deal with the same essential issues that Feng Shui addresses: the pursuit of health, prosperity, and happiness.

KITCHENS

Food symbolizes health and wealth in Feng Shui. When money is flowing, we can afford to buy the best food to sustain good health. When we are in good health, we are best able to make a good living. Because food bridges the two treasures of health and wealth, special attention is given to the place where food is prepared—the kitchen.

The stove, typically the center for food preparation, needs to be kept very clean. Use all the burners regularly, symbolizing the full circulation of prosperity.

If the stove is located next to the kitchen sink, place a healthy plant, flowers, or bowl of fruit between them to represent the Wood element, thus balancing the elemental relationship between sink (Water) and stove (Fire).

When the stove is placed against a wall, put a reflective surface behind or beside it, such as a mirror or shiny metal tray. The reflection "doubles" the burners (and the health and wealth they represent), and gives cooks a view of what's going on behind them.

Keep your knives completely out of sight when not in use.

KITCHENS, CONT'D.

 Declutter kitchen countertops. Take an honest look at what's living on your counters. Do you use everything there every day? If not, put away the items you don't regularly use. Avoid the temptation to pile mail and you-name-it on the counters. Make plenty of room for meals to be enjoyably prepared and for the Ch'i to flow.

 Place trash and recycling containers out of sight. If these containers are currently "homeless," decide how you can rearrange cabinets or pantries to accommodate them.

 Entering and exiting the house through the kitchen can promote an eternal appetite. Consider using another door as your primary entrance, or screen the refrigerator from first sight.

INNER WORK—*To maintain abundant flow of inner health and prosperity, it is vital to nourish your spirit on a daily basis. Make a list of the experiences that nourish your soul, and feast with gusto upon one or more each day.*

Every square inch of your house is important in Feng Shui.

LAUNDRY ROOMS

Laundry rooms often fall into the same category of "non-room" as hallways, storage rooms, garages, basements, and attics. Because every square inch of your house is important in Feng Shui, it's essential that your laundry room be as welcoming as the rest of your home.

If you normally enter and exit your home through your garage and laundry room, you have a second foyer of sorts. Make it openly welcoming rather than a constant reminder of chores. House your washer and dryer—and all paraphernalia that goes with them—in a closet or behind a curtain that can be closed between uses.

Because a laundry room entrance is more private than your official front entrance, you can be whimsical or offbeat there. You may want to paint the laundry room a bright color, or wallpaper it in sports memorabilia, travel posters, or children's art. Decorate it with whatever welcomes you home and makes you feel good there! Install a chandelier, hang a fabulous mirror, or paint a mural on the walls. The point is to make sure you feel welcome every time you open the laundry room door.

Make your laundry room a place you enjoy.

 Even when your laundry room isn't an entrance, make it a place where you enjoy spending time.

LIBRARIES

Most homes do not have an official library. Yet, many of us have books—lots and lots of books! Just like everything else, they need a wonderful place to live where we can see and enjoy them.

 Your books should reflect your current interests. Sort through them and decide which books are no longer important to you. They are always welcome at your local library or secondhand book store.

Your books need a home. Your needs may be met with one or two bookshelves, or you may need to convert a den or guest room into a full-fledged library.

All books need a place to be read. Locate a comfortable chair or seating near your bookshelves, and make sure there is ample lighting for reading.

LIGHTING

Lighting can greatly enhance the Ch'i in our homes. Options include incandescent and halogen electric lights, candles (see page 27), oil lamps, fireplaces (see page 65), and natural sunlight.

When building, consider your electric lighting needs, inside and out. Soffits, wall sconces, canned lights, and track lighting are easiest to install during the building process. Locate electrical outlets in the floors of active rooms so that you won't need to run wires across the floors later.

Improve Ch'i flow through your home by illuminating dark corners, camouflaging sharp angles, and warming gloomy rooms with lighting. Consider leaving low-wattage lights on all or most of the time in rooms with no natural light.

LIGHTING, CONT'D.

 Use lighting to symbolically complete and enhance "missing" areas, indoors and out (see the Bagua Map, page 131).

Avoid fluorescent lights. Both standard and "stick-up" varieties flicker, buzz audibly, and emit only part of the light spectrum, giving everyone a sickly pallor and depleting the environment of Ch'i. Although full-spectrum fluorescent bulbs are better, they still buzz and flicker. Disconnect or replace fluorescent fixtures especially when located directly overhead, and rely or incandescent, halogen, and natural lighting.

 Lighting can be artistic, so choose fixtures that you love! Collect lamps that add personality to your decor. Let the light that fills your home be a reflection of your taste and creative expression.

Use as many night lights as necessary to make your home safe. Install them as needed in hallways, stairways, bathrooms, and closets.

LIVING ROOMS

The living room is usually the first room you see when you walk through the front door of a home. It's meant for "living," and symbolizes your public, social self. Concentrate on making it warm and welcoming. Display the art, colors, collections, and interests that you enjoy. Whether it's Tiffany lamps, photographs, or handcrafted furniture, show your world who you are and what turns you on.

As you make changes in your environment, you may tire of your color scheme and want to modify it. With this in mind, consider neutral tones for your large pieces of furniture. They then become backdrops for colorful art and decor that you can vary as you change.

To encourage social intimacy, comfort, and safety, it's important that you arrange your furniture with care. Place your primary seating—a sofa for instance—in an area that allows you to see the door when sitting there. Or, hang a mirror to reflect the door from the sofa. Arrange other seating, such as love seats and chairs, so that you have at least a peripheral view of the door.

Check your furniture for sharp corners and other dangers. If you have glass, wood, or metal furniture with "unfriendly" features or corners, either soften them with fabric, or turn at a diagonal to lessen the danger. As you buy new furniture, put safety and comfort first by choosing pieces that don't have sharp corners or threatening features.

Put electronic equipment, such as televisions and stereos, into cabinets with doors. This will enhance both conversation when other people are with you, and serenity when you are alone.

INNER WORK—*Consider whether you are as friendly and kind to yourself as you are to your friends. Do you treat yourself like an honored and welcome guest—with kindness, love, and respect? Your inner health and happiness is enhanced when you treat yourself as you would an honored guest. Dr. Christiane Northrup, author of* Women's Bodies, Women's Wisdom, *has a wonderful affirmation she recommends that we say at least twice a day: "I UNCONDITIONALLY LOVE AND HONOR MYSELF, JUST THE WAY I AM, RIGHT NOW." Live with this attitude, and you'll strengthen your ability to love yourself and others.*

MIRRORS

Mirrors activate, expand, and circulate Ch'i throughout interior spaces. When properly chosen and installed, they can visually enlarge small rooms, double beautiful views, and enhance a sense of safety and comfort.

Mirrors make a room more active. They're great when you want to keep the Ch'i lively in rooms such as the living room, family room, office, bathroom, and kitchen, but they are not meant for rooms dedicated to sleep and relaxation. Use them to "cure" or erase architectural challenges such as poles and odd angles, or to enhance positive features such as a great view. In general, the bigger, the better!

One of the quickest ways to calm a bedroom down (along with its occupants) is to remove or cover the mirrors (see Bedrooms, page 13). You can treat large mirrors like windows, with beautiful curtains or shades that can be opened by day and closed by night. Other mirrors can be moved to a more active room or draped with fabric at night. This is especially important if the bedroom's occupants are not sleeping well there.

MIRRORS, CONT'D.

Mirrors can overactivate the dining room and influence diners to hurry through their meals (see Dining Rooms, page 51).

It is crucial in Feng Shui to choose mirrors that reflect whole, realistic images. Clear, bright mirrors reflect clear, bright Ch'i; therefore mirrors that are one clean, clear piece of glass are best (they can be beveled around the outside edges). Avoid mirrors that distort or cut up images, as they distort and break up the Ch'i. These include mirrors made from many beveled pieces, broken or mottled mirrors, and mirrored tiles. And, always keep your mirror crystal clean.

Make sure each mirror in the house is hung high enough to reflect every adult's entire head with several inches to spare. This requires that mirrors be large enough or high enough to accommodate everyone's height. Mirrors that reflect your whole image enhance your self-esteem, whereas reflections that cut your head off have the opposite effect.

Mirrors are wonderful for opening up small spaces.

 What do your mirrors reflect? Are they enhancing the harmony in the room by reflecting something beautiful? If you have a mirror that's reflecting an eyesore, either change the placement of the mirror or beautify the reflection.

Mirrors hung directly across from each other reflect images to infinity, distorting and disorienting people and Ch'i.

Mirrors are wonderful for opening up small spaces that would otherwise feel confining. Hung directly across from hall doors, or any door in close quarters, they make the wall "disappear" and give the impression of more space. Mirrors hung across from windows will increase the light, as well as the perceived size of small foyers, dens, and home offices.

Use mirrors to reflect what's behind you when your back is to the door—when you're sitting at your computer, for example.

In Feng Shui, mirrors are sometimes used to push energy back from whence it came. If you have a very unsightly view of power lines, sharp corners from other buildings, or an impossible neighbor, you can hang a small mirror that *faces* in their direction. It can be placed over a window or door outside, or behind a painting or under a rug inside. Always point the reflective side of the mirror *toward* the offender. Hang it in the spirit of goodwill, with the intention of redirecting the energy and improving the Ch'i. Any mirror that is about two inches wide (such as a compact mirror) can be used.

NATURE OBJECTS

Nature objects can be very Ch'i-enhancing when they connect you to the special experiences you've had outdoors. Bowls of shells, baskets of pine cones, vases of seed pods; and collections of rocks, stones, and fossils can be the most evocative mementos, especially if you gathered them yourself. The memories associated with your nature objects keep

Nature objects can connect you to special experiences you've had outdoors.

you connected to the natural world, even when you live in an urban setting. And unlike plants, flowers, and pets, nature objects are "easy-care," requiring only an occasional cleaning.

OFFICES (IN THE HOME)

Your home office should be a place of power. This is where you run your personal empire, and what occurs here leads directly to your success in the world. If your work is action oriented, your office is best located near the front of the house. If your work is more contemplative, your ideal location is toward the back. Either way, make sure you have the privacy you need from household activities. Give your home office the same attention you give your best client or biggest project. It's your worldly battery—keep it fully charged!

Make sure you're sitting in the room's most powerful "command" position. You want to see the door and yet not be sitting directly in front of it. It's also best to have a wall, not a window, behind you.

OFFICES, CONT'D.

This keeps you tucked into the room, solidly supported from the back, with a commanding view from the front. If you have a window behind you, put plants, shades, or furniture there as a buffer between you and the window. And when you can't sit facing the door, place a mirror on or behind your desk to reflect the door.

Being organized in your home office is critical. Powerful, productive Ch'i cannot find its way through piles of papers, files, and office equipment (see Chaos, page 32). Become the "samurai of clutter"—decide what organizing strategy works for you, and stick to it. Your productivity will skyrocket!

If you find yourself hip-deep in chaos with no way out, don't despair. Hire a professional organizer to set up systems to keep you organized and productive.

Make sure your office chair is the most comfortable chair in your universe.

This is the place for powerful art and colors that represent your contributions to the world. What are the images and colors that match your professional goals and aspirations? Choose art and colors that summon your power and keep you inspired.

Sharp angles and corners promote irritation and aggression, so camouflage or soften them (see Angles, page 1). When buying new furniture, choose designs with rounded corners. Circular and oval tables are best for sustaining harmony in meetings.

Make sure your "throne" (your office chair) is the most comfortable chair in your universe. It should have great lumbar support, be solid, and fit your body in every way. "Test-drive" desk chairs that rock back and forth from a stable five-legged base and have adjustable headrests and armrests.

When choosing your desk or work table, assess your needs carefully before deciding on size and design. Do you need one large surface or several smaller surfaces? What height? How will the

desk interact with your chair? Do you like to stand, sit, or move around when you work? How much equipment will share the desk with you? Many desks now have hidden openings to drop electrical wires through and keep them under control. When working with an existing desk that's placed out in the middle of the room, make sure to either hide wires behind screens, plants, or furniture, or have a "false front" made so that wires fall between your desk and an attractive new panel. Always run wires safely under a carpet or area rug, or install appropriate outlets near your desk.

INNER WORK—*Do you believe in yourself? Do you hold the vision of being a great success? Have you clearly defined your purpose in life? Meditate on how to align your purpose in life with your professional goals. Post affirmations that keep you inspired, such as "EVERYTHING I TOUCH IS A SUCCESS," and "EVERY DAY MY WORK ATTRACTS MAGNIFICENT PEOPLE AND OPPORTUNITIES INTO MY LIFE."*

Meditate on how to align your purpose in life with your professional goals.

Everything is alive with Ch'i.

PHILOSOPHY OF FENG SHUI

The foundation of Feng Shui is built on three basic principles:

1. *Everything Is Alive with Ch'i*

The first principle in the Feng Shui philosophy is that every person, place, and thing is alive with Ch'i, or vital energy (see Ch'i, page 36). Along with being molecularly alive, our material possessions are subjectively alive with our thoughts, feelings, and associations. This concept is all-inclusive and tends to throw a monkey wrench into how we've viewed the world to date. It changes our physical existence from a world "that" is largely inanimate to a world "who" is completely alive.

When we see our world as made up of animate "beings," rather than a bunch of inanimate "stuff," we make different choices. Clear-cutting and bulldozing areas to bang up as many houses as possible can only happen when we believe none of it is really alive. When we feel the aliveness of all things around us, including the earth beneath our feet, we tend to take good care of them. We slow down, build around the knees and elbows of the land, and work in harmony with "who's" already living there. We also choose our belongings much more carefully, knowing that everything is imbued with living energy that can build us up or break us down. We want to be surrounded by possessions "who" strengthen our sense of well-being all the time.

Every "thing" that lives with you evokes certain memories, associations, and feelings. That's why it's important in Feng Shui to assess your material possessions. What are they "saying" to you? The quality of your inner life is constantly influenced by what you're keeping alive in your surroundings. Your feelings and memories may be of good times and delicious moments, a mixed combination of associations, or they may be quite negative.

In Feng Shui, one of your primary goals is to surround yourself with "environmental affirmations," or the things who are alive with life-affirming associations. When you design your environment to affirm your life, you are opening the pathways for happiness, health, and prosperity to take up residence with you, and you're creating your environment to be your personal paradise.

Everything is connected by Ch'i.

INNER WORK—*Look around and choose something that belongs to you. It could be your watch, your shirt, the chair you're sitting on, or a nearby piece of art. As you focus on that one object, what comes to mind? A rich medley of feelings, memories, and associations may come up—for example, when you bought or received it, what the occasion was, whether it was a good deal, who was there, and so on. Ask, "Do the thoughts and feelings this object is alive with strengthen or weaken my sense of well-being?" If, in fact, it weakens your sense of well-being, are you willing, ready, and able to let it go?*

2. *Everything Is Connected by Ch'i*

The second basic principle of Feng Shui is that every person, place, and thing is connected by Ch'i. Although our connections are usually strongest with the people, places, and things that are close by, we are essentially in relationship with everyone and everything on Earth.

Conflicting relationships can diminish or damage the quality of Ch'i in our lives. When we recognize that we cannot isolate ourselves, we see

Philosophy of Feng Shui, cont'd.

the importance of resolving our conflicts and cultivating good relationships. Because everything is connected, resolving relationship problems greatly improves the overall quality of our lives.

We are also intimately connected to every single "thing" that surrounds us. And, in our culture, most of us have thousands of *things!* So in the spirit of good relationship, it's crucial to simplify, organize, and properly house our possessions—including the ones in garages, basements, attics, and closets. As Victoria Moran says in her book *Shelter for the Spirit*: "If you organize before you simplify, things will be disorganized again in no time. This is not because you are a hopeless slob without a prayer of redemption. It is because excess cannot be organized. If it could, it wouldn't be excess."

This doesn't mean that you suddenly have to live a deprived existence, because material well-being tends to increase in the presence of order. Simply let go of anything you don't have a great relationship with, remembering that external order and harmony create internal harmony and clarity.

In the same way, the many aspects of our lives are interconnected. We cannot separate our health from our finances, our finances from our creativity, or our creativity from our relationships. Every part of our life is

Change becomes a gift when we embrace it as a force that can improve our lives.

connected to all the other parts. Change or remove one part and the whole picture is altered. For instance, your job will take a toll on your physical vitality and general outlook on life if it's stressful. On the other hand, if you love your work, you'll find that your relationships, health, creativity, and passion for life are all strengthened as a result.

INNER WORK—*Take a few moments to consider whether you have some unfriendly connections with yourself or others. Your outer environment may include neighbors you dislike, alienated family members, or co-workers who are troublesome. Knowing how connected you are to other people, it's time to reinstate harmony and balance in all relationships, including your relationship with yourself. Contemplate the meaning of healthy relationships, and practice generosity, compassion, honesty, and forgiveness, knowing that the quality of your life depends on it.*

"If you want a change in your life, move 27 things in your house."

PHILOSOPHY OF FENG SHUI, CONT'D.

3. The Ch'i in Everything Is Changing

The third Feng Shui principle states that the Ch'i in every person, place, and thing is constantly changing. In fact, the one constant in our physical universe is change. And it becomes a gift when we embrace it as a force that can improve our lives.

Embracing change is often resisted in our Western culture. We want to look 25 forever, buy furniture only once, and have one career that lasts a lifetime. As we all know, life doesn't work that way. Change happens. As we grow older and hopefully wiser, we may marry, have children, divorce, change careers, move, make new friends, remarry, and through it all, experience tremendous inner and outer changes. When we fully join the dance of change and "let it happen," we grow in wisdom and experience, and we allow our homes to reflect our changes.

For instance, you may change careers and turn a guest room into a home office, or transform the master bedroom into your art studio. As you change, you might want more yellow in your living room or purple in your bedroom. You may feel compelled to add built-in storage, an exercise area, or an atrium for your collection of orchids. When you feel the need to change something about your home, do your best to follow through as quickly as possible. Changing your living space anchors and supports the newest you, while the lack of change keeps the old you in place.

There's a Chinese saying: "If you want a change in your life, move 27 things in your house." When you alter your home in a positive way, you bring positive changes into your life. Feng Shui invites you to embrace change, lighten up, and let your environment grow and move with you. To help you change, install casters on heavy furniture such as desks and sofas so you can easily move things around. Any change you make doesn't need to last forever. Let your creativity run a little wild, and enjoy the moment, knowing that it's all going to change anyway!

INNER WORK—*If you could change anything about your inner relation-ship with yourself, what would it be? Perhaps you have a tendency to be stingy and judgmental with yourself. If this is so, now is the time to become more generous and forgiving. To environmentally affirm your positive change, you could place an abundant arrangement of fresh flowers in your living room, symbolizing generosity and self-love. Affirm your inner change by saying, "I AM ALWAYS CHANGING FOR THE BETTER. CHANGE BRINGS MAGNIFICENT INNER AND OUTER EXPERIENCES INTO MY LIFE. I EMBRACE CHANGE, AND CHANGE LOVINGLY EMBRACES ME."*

PLANTS

Plants are superb Ch'i enhancers when they are healthy and vibrant. They are used in Feng Shui to enhance and improve Ch'i quality and to solve many architectural problems. They also provide us with the most fundamental enhancement . . . cleaning the air around us.

Choose "friendly" plants, such as those with wide, rounded leaves or a generally soft, graceful appearance. There are many varieties of plants that fall into this category, including schefflera, philodendron, pothos, jade, croton, Chinese evergreen (aglaonema), peace lily (spathiphyllum), ficus, ivy, and most draceanas, ferns, and palms. Also on the "yes" list are blooming plants, which are excellent alternatives to fresh flowers. These include begonia, chrysanthemum, gloxinia, African violet, kalanchoe, Gerbera daisy, and cyclamen.

"Unfriendly" plants with a sharp or spiky appearance should be used only when located away from people. These include draceana marginata, sago palm, yucca, and most cacti and bromeliads.

Plants soften the hard angles and sharp corners found in furnishings and architecture. Use vining plants such as pothos or ivy to camouflage sharp corners on furniture. Soften sharp angles projecting into rooms, and fill in corners and unusable spaces with healthy plants. Make sure the plants you choose and the available lighting complement each other.

Consider using silk plants in areas that are dark, high, or untended for long periods of time. As long as they look vibrantly alive, silk plants are a viable alternative to living plants. Bend branches and leaves to give them a more natural appearance. Silk plants tend to last longer than silk flowers (see Flowers, page 66), about 18 to 24 months. Dust and clean with silk plant cleaner on a regular basis.

PLANTS, CONT'D.

When a plant becomes diseased, infested, or unsightly, it's best to "give it back to God" and replace it. Don't try to nurse a plant back to health unless you have a greenhouse or area specifically set up for this. Healthy, vibrant plants improve the Ch'i; unhealthy ones do not.

Place your plants in beautiful containers and pots. Make their container "homes" pleasing to the eye and the spirit, and make sure to protect your floors and furniture from water spills with waterproof saucers or mats.

When a plant becomes diseased, infested, or unsightly, it's best to "give it back to God" and replace it.

Sound makers can lift people's moods, transforming stress or lethargy into a more harmonious, energized state.

SOUND MAKERS

Wind chimes, bells, bead curtains, and gongs summon and protect harmonious Ch'i. Their lovely sounds can also signal someone's approach, enhancing our sense of safety. They can subtly mark the boundary between one area and another, such as between living and dining rooms or front yards and foyers. When chosen for their melodious tones, sound makers, including music and musical instruments, can also lift people's moods, transforming stress or lethargy into a more harmonious, energized state.

STAIRWAYS

Consider stairways with a critical eye. Likened to waterfalls of rushing Ch'i, their location plays an important role in how Ch'i flows through your home. The least favored placement is directly in front of the main entrance to a home. The longer and steeper the stairs, the greater their tendency to whisk Ch'i too quickly down and out the door.

 When building a home, locate stairways away from doors, especially the front door. Make the stairs wide and gracious, and include curves and landings to soften the descending flow.

 If you have a stairway that faces the front entrance of your home, you'll need to temper the flow of Ch'i pouring out the door. The best way is to place a barrier between the staircase and the front door. This could be anything that's pleasing and in scale with the space, such as a table with flowers, or any combination of sculpture, screens, banners, or plants. Make sure your choice does not crowd your front entrance area.

When there is no room to place anything between the stairs and the door, hang a mirror directly across from the stairs to symbolically catch the descending Ch'i and reflect it back up the stairs. Or, you can hang a faceted crystal (see Crystals, page 45) above the bottom step to help lift and circulate the falling Ch'i.

Don't "step" your art down a staircase, as this only accentuates the descent. Instead, group pieces together to form a strong horizontal line to visually adjust and balance the descent of the stairs.

Hang a crystal above a bottom step to lift and circulate the Ch'i.

W
to
Z

WATER FEATURES

Water features invigorate Ch'i flow. You will find many indoor and outdoor varieties in department stores, nurseries, and catalogs, or you can make your own one-of-a-kind water feature.

Aquariums are highly prized Ch'i enhancers, as they gather the five elements of Wood (plants), Fire (fish), Earth (sand), Metal (rocks), and Water into one dynamic feature. When maintained properly, they attract prosperity into your home or business.

Whether inside or outside, place directional water features so that the water "points" toward the house or into the room. Still-water features such as birdbaths and urns also enhance Ch'i flow when kept crystal clean.

123

WATER FEATURES, CONT'D.

Pools, Jacuzzis, and hot tubs are considered water features and must be kept clean, well lit, in good repair, and in many cases, fenced for safety. When designing these features, "amp" them up by including a waterfall flowing toward your house, and Ch'i-enhancing touches of good lighting, bright flowers, and comfortable seating nearby.

INNER WORK—*Water features symbolize rich, abundant amounts of Ch'i flowing through your life. Are you paying attention to all the riches that flow to you on a daily basis? Riches come in myriad forms, from loving friends and family, warm sunshine, and contentment with the moment, to a healthy body and a delicious meal. Money is just one of the ways in which wealth and prosperity appear in your life. One of best ways to increase your sense of prosperity is to begin a Gratitude Journal, where before bed each night you can write down what you were grateful for that day. As Catherine Ponder says in her book*

Wind dancers beckon, uplift, and invigorate the Ch'i that circulates through our homes.

The Dynamic Laws of Prosperity, *"The attitude of gratitude keeps prosperity coming to me from every direction."*

WIND DANCERS

Wind dancers such as whirligigs, weather vanes, mobiles, prayer flags, and banners serve to beckon, uplift, and invigorate the Ch'i that circulates through our homes. Outdoors, they act as friendly landmarks and symbolically lift the Ch'i when placed on low roof lines and steep slopes. Inside, they help to balance extreme features such as beams (page 10) and high ceilings (page 27) with their soft, inviting presence.

WINDOWS

Windows are considered the "eyes" of the house. They bring light and views into your home, and their placement and treatment is important when adjusting the Ch'i flow through the house.

Views are often more enticing when "discovered" rather than immediately apparent.

WINDOWS, CONT'D.

When building, it's best not to line up a window and a door (see Doors, page 54) directly across from each other, especially a large picture window with an awesome view. This tends to create a pathway between the two that pulls the Ch'i too quickly across and out of the room. Attractive as it may be, it can easily leave the room "undernourished." Ideally, we—as well as the Ch'i—have a moment to adjust and settle into a room before we're pulled through to the other side. Views are often more enticing when "discovered" rather than immediately apparent.

When you have a large window and a door lined up directly across from each other, place something between them, such as an aquarium, sculpture, plants, or flowers to slow and redirect the Ch'i. Or, you can soften the window itself with curtains or blinds. Furniture, plants, and art placed near the window can also help

catch and recirculate some of the Ch'i passing through the room. When there is no space for these things, hang a round, faceted crystal between window and door (see Crystals, page 45) to help circulate the Ch'i throughout the room.

Check the view you have from every window (and door) in your home. What do you see? If you love what you see, great. If you don't, decide what you can do to improve the view (see Gardens, page 76). If you're looking straight into a fence, hang something wonderful on the fence, plant something green and lush in front of it, or paint it a beautiful color. If you look out on a parking lot, shutter the bottom half of the window, and let the light flood in from above, or hang bird feeders and blooming plants just outside the window. If your view is a lawn leading to a busy street, landscape specifically to enhance the view from the house. Highlight views with birdbaths, sculptures, and other "beauty marks" that you may not be able to see from any other place.

When views are impossible to enhance, or for privacy after dark, fit all your windows with appropriate coverings.

When windows are smaller than you would like, use beautiful lamps and bright or light colors in the room to enhance and reflect the available light. Place a mirror or art with reflective glass across from the window to increase the natural light.

 As with mirrors, it's best to install large single-paned windows, rather than those with many small panes. Glass that was designed to be art, such as stained glass windows, can be as ornate and segmented as you'd like.

 Skylights are recommended in active rooms such as living rooms, dens, offices, family rooms, kitchens, garages, and bathrooms; but not directly over your bed, desk, or dining table. Skylights tend to activate the upward flow of Ch'i, making it difficult to sit or rest. If you already have a skylight over a piece of furniture, rearrange the furniture, or install a shade so that you can adjust it as necessary.

 All windows should be kept clean and in good repair. This includes windows in garages, basements, attics, and other out-of-the-way places.

BAGUA MAP

WEALTH & PROSPERITY "Gratitude" **REAR LEFT** Blues, purples, and reds	**FAME & REPUTATION** "Integrity" **REAR MIDDLE** Fire Reds	**LOVE & MARRIAGE** "Receptivity" **REAR RIGHT** Reds, pinks, and whites
HEALTH & FAMILY "Strength" **MIDDLE LEFT** Blues and greens	**CENTER** "Earth" Yellow and earthtones	**CREATIVITY & CHILDREN** "Joy" **MIDDLE RIGHT** Metal White and pastels
KNOWLEDGE & SELF-CULTIVATION "Stillness" **FRONT LEFT** Black, blues, and greens	**CAREER** "Depth" **FRONT MIDDLE** Water Black and darktones	**HELPFUL PEOPLE & TRAVEL** "Synchronicity" **FRONT RIGHT** White, gray, and black

↑ ↑ ↑

FRONT ENTRANCE

WEALTH & PROSPERITY "Gratitude" **REAR LEFT** Blues, purples, and reds	**FAME & REPUTATION** "Integrity" **REAR MIDDLE** Fire Reds	**LOVE & MARRIAGE** "Receptivity" **REAR RIGHT** Reds, pinks, and whites
HEALTH & FAMILY "Strength" **MIDDLE LEFT** Blues and greens	**CENTER** "Earth" Yellow and earthtones	**CREATIVITY & CHILDREN** "Joy" **MIDDLE RIGHT** Metal White and pastels
KNOWLEDGE & SELF-CULTIVATION "Stillness" **FRONT LEFT** Black, blues, and greens	**CAREER** "Depth" **FRONT MIDDLE** Water Black and darktones	**HELPFUL PEOPLE & TRAVEL** "Synchronicity" **FRONT RIGHT** White, gray, and black

FRONT ENTRANCE

THE BAGUA MAP

One of the most exciting aspects of Feng Shui is the Bagua Map. Based on the *I Ching*—the Chinese Book of Changes—Bagua literally means "Eight (Ba) Trigram (Gua)," and describes the eight basic building blocks of the *I Ching*. In Feng Shui, the Bagua Map connects the design of your home with the blessings and treasures of life.

People have solved many "unsolvable" problems in their lives by mapping the Bagua of their homes. They may find that their Wealth and Prosperity Gua correlates with a chaotic area in their garage, or that their Fame and Reputation Gua is located on a back porch filled with dead plants. They may also discover that all Guas need to be cleared of chaos and unwanted possessions. When they clean out the disorganized and unloved places in their homes, positive results are assured.

The best way to achieve the most positive results when using the Bagua Map is to seek external improvement of your environment, as well as development of your inner self. As you enhance a Gua's physical location in your home, also take into consideration the associated inner work. When you cultivate the domain where your mind, heart, and spirit dwell, you complete the circle and attract many blessings into your life. Your inner "home improvements," coupled with your outer Feng Shui work, produce the most deeply satisfying and long-lasting results.

Inner Work Relating to the Bagua Map

 HEALTH AND FAMILY—As you are enhancing the Health and Family Gua of your home, also seek to strengthen the well-being of your heart and soul. Find the places within you that want to grow and expand, and allow them to flower, while building a strong sense of self-esteem. This inner work can create vibrant health on all levels, Concentrate on healing relationships with your family and friends so that they are healthy, honest, and loving.

WEALTH AND PROSPERITY—When working with the Wealth and Prosperity Gua, also give your attention to cultivating a strong feeling of gratitude for all of the riches in your life. Honor everyone and everything you have been blessed with. Gratitude leads to the steadfast experience of physical, emotional, mental, and spiritual prosperity.

FAME AND REPUTATION—When enhancing the Fame and Reputation Gua of your home, focus on honing the qualities of integrity, and authenticity. These qualities illuminate your path, enhance your recognition in your community, and attract many positive opportunities into your life.

LOVE AND MARRIAGE—As you are improving your Love and Marriage Gua, also concentrate on building unconditional love for yourself and others. Allow your intuition and inner truth to guide you in life. Practice fully receiving and enjoying the goodness held in each day.

CHILDREN AND CREATIVITY—When enhancing the Children and Creativity Gua, focus on also cultivating the qualities of childlike joy and openness to pleasure. Encourage creativity to flow from within yourself and others in all its benevolent forms. By doing so, you'll recognize the small miracles inherent in every moment and enjoy a playful, creative life.

HELPFUL PEOPLE AND TRAVEL—When improving the Helpful People and Travel Gua in your home, also take the time to clearly define your spiritual beliefs. Hone the qualities of self-empowerment and confidence. Be purposeful in all your actions, and you'll find that synchronicity—harmonious happenings beyond your ability to plan—occur in your life on a daily basis, making your life "Heaven on Earth."

CAREER—As you work with your Career Gua, contemplate your willingness to connect deeply with your soul and follow your bliss. Practice trusting your personal journey and being comfortable with the mysteries of life. These inner qualities support the perfect unfolding and fulfillment of your' life's destiny.

KNOWLEDGE AND SELF-CULTIVATION—When enhancing the Knowledge and Self-Cultivation Gua of your home, also attend to your own tranquility. Practice some form of introspection or meditation on a daily basis; nurture yourself with stillness and silence. Cultivate inner peace in the presence of outer activity. As you do, life becomes calmer, and a deep and abiding wisdom unfolds within you.

CENTER—When working with the Center of the Bagua Map, determine how grounded you feel in your life. Nurture your ability to remain centered through life's many changes. Find a way to connect with the earth every day. By doing so, your life naturally revolves around a strong, grounded inner core that is centered deep within you.

Mapping the Bagua of Your Home

The Bagua Map can be applied to any fixed shape, including buildings, rooms, and furniture. These instructions are geared toward mapping your home, and once you understand the basics, you can use them on any structure. You will need a bird's-eye drawing of your home, such as a blueprint or footprint sketch. Determine the overall shape of your home, including all parts that are *attached* to the main house, such as garages, porches, room additions, arbors, storage huts, and decks with railings.

Lay the drawing down so that the front entrance of your house is at the bottom of the page. (See Bagua map and examples that follow). Now, draw a rectangle around your home just big enough to include every part of the home inside it. This is the outline of your Bagua Map. Divide the outline into nine even sections, like a Tic-Tac-Toe board, and label the nine squares according to the Bagua Map on page 131. This is your complete Bagua Map.

When your home is a simple rectangle, you will find that all of the Bagua areas are located inside the structure of your house. If your home is any other shape, such as an L, S, T, or U, you'll find areas that are located within the rectangular outline of the Bagua Map, but outside the structure of your house. Whether indoors or outdoors, it's very important to determine each "Gua's" location.

Examples of Applying the Bagua Map to Buildings

1) When applying the Bagua Map, we find that the front entrance is located in the Helpful People and Travel area. We also find that this building is "missing" the Wealth and Prosperity area, which is located outside of the physical structure of the building.

W&P	F&R	L&M
H&F	CENTER	C&C
K&SC	C	HP&T

Front Entrance

2) This rectangular building has its front entrance located in the Knowledge and Self-Cultivation area, and has all the Bagua areas inside its physical structure.

W&P	F&R	L&M
H&F	CENTER	C&C
K&SC	C	HP&T

Front Entrance

3) This building has its front entrance located in the Career area of the Bagua Map. Also, both the Wealth and Prosperity and the Love and Marriage areas of the Bagua are "missing," or outside of this building's physical structure.

W&P	F&R	L&M
H&F	CENTER	C&C
K&SC	C	HP&T

Front Entrance

4) This recessed front entrance actually enters through the Center of this building. This leaves the Career area of the Bagua "missing," or outside of the physical structure of the building.

W&P	F&R	L&M
H&F	CENTER	C&C
K&SC	C	HP&T

Front Entrance

——— = Building   - - - - - - = Bagua Map

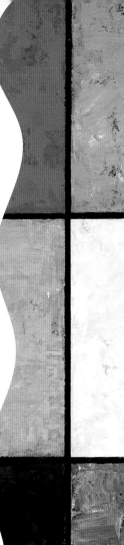

Clarifying Points:

1. Don't be concerned with where the walls are inside the house. Sometimes one large room will divide into two or three Guas, or one Gua might encompass two or three small rooms.

2. If your home has more than one story, *partial or full*, the Bagua Map of the main floor will translate directly up to a second story or down to a lower level. Multiple floors give you multiple opportunities to enhance the Bagua.

3. When the door of your front entrance is built on a diagonal, you will have to "make a call" as to which way to place the Bagua Map on the house. You may have an immediate feeling and intuitively know which way to place the Map. Sometimes, the direction in which tile or carpet has been installed determine the Bagua's direction. Other times, the direction you see when you first open the door is the determining factor.

4. When your front door is recessed past the front wall of the house, you may be entering your home through the Health and Family, Center, or Children and Creativity areas of the Bagua Map (see example #4, page 135). If your front door is extremely recessed so that it opens into Wealth and Prosperity, Fame and Reputation, or Love and Marriage, turn the Bagua Map to fit over the main body of the house.

5. Because the home is larger than each room, it holds more Chi. Therefore, work first with the Bagua Map of the home, then with each room.

6. Consult a Feng Shui practitioner if you need help making a Bagua Map of your home.

Missing Areas of the Bagua Map

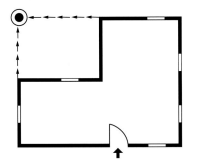

When there are Bagua areas outside the physical structure of your home, define and enhance them in some way. This can be as simple as installing an outdoor lamp post, ornamental tree, or large statue where the corner would be if the structure were rectangular.

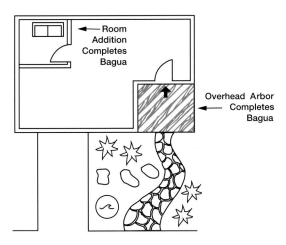

Room Addition Completes Bagua

Overhead Arbor Completes Bagua

Or, it can be a much larger project, such as filling in the missing area with a deck, patio, arbor, or room addition. The goal is to anchor or complete the missing area with something significant that's in scale and in harmony with your home.

Simple enhancements such as flagpoles, large boulders, trees, fences, water features, lights, or outdoor sculptures can be combined to complete the missing Gua. This, in turn, increases the Ch'i flow in and around your home.

Personalizing Your Choices

Whenever you can, choose items and designs that relate to the individual Gua you are working with. If your Love and Marriage area is missing, you can create a romantic garden that includes two flowering trees and a bench that seats two people. When enhancing the Health and Family area outside, you could plant a variety of healing herbs and include a table and chairs to encourage family and friends to spend time outdoors. There is no end to the creative possibilities as you build the Ch'i to enhance the quality of your life.

When You Can't Do Anything BIG Outside

Don't be discouraged if you can't do anything substantial to complete the Bagua on the outside of your home. There are still many ways you can complete a missing Gua by working with it symbolically outside, inside, or both.

Symbolic Enhancements

 Missing Guas can be marked and symbolically strengthened by "planting" a natural quartz crystal at the corner of an absent Gua.

Bury the crystal, point up, an inch or two below the ground with the intention of restoring and completing the Ch'i flow. Your intention empowers the crystal to energetically strengthen and support the Gua that is missing in structure.

Mark pavement that covers the missing area with a painted line, circle, or artistic mural. This can be used wherever cement covers a missing Gua. Again, your intention to positively influence the flow of Ch'i combined with your physical act of marking the spot makes your symbol powerful.

Indoors, hang a large mirror on the wall closest to the missing Gua. This symbolically opens up the wall to include the Gua.

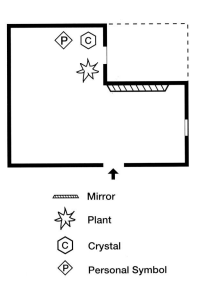

Or, hang a faceted crystal in the window located near the missing area. Use any of the Ch'i Enhancers (see page 95) to power up the windows and walls located closest to the missing Gua.

Make sure that when a Gua is missing in your home's structure, you enhance it in each room of the house.

Mirror
Plant
Crystal
Personal Symbol

Mapping the Bagua in Every Room

Follow the same steps when mapping a room as you did mapping your house. Draw the footprint of the room, place the main door into the room at the bottom of the page, draw a rectangle around the perimeter, divide it into nine equal parts, and label each section according to the Bagua Map.

Please note that the Bagua Map of your home and the Bagua Map of each room are usually *not* going to coincide. Each room has its own smaller Map, with its own possibilities for enhancement. You'll have the Bagua Map of your home, plus different smaller Maps for each room.

Assessing Your Bagua Map Profile

Take some time to check out each Bagua area of your home. First look at the home's Bagua Map, then at each room's Map, and answer the following questions:

 What room or area is located in each Gua?

 What possessions are located there?

 Are they organized?

 Do I love everything I see?

 Do I see a correlation between what's located in the Gua and the quality of my life?

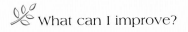 What can I improve?

 What is the first Bagua area I'm going to work with?

This can be a very revealing process! We often find that the condition of the Bagua areas in our homes matches up with the places of harmony in our lives, as well as any places of stress or strain. A woman I know whose only complaint was that she couldn't stop smoking realized she had a pencil cactus flourishing in her Health and Family area. Each section of cactus was the length and width of a cigarette. The cactus's container was appointed with a beautiful red wooden carving of a flame. This happens all the time. The objects we surround ourselves with on a daily basis are either nurturing us or not. If they're not, they may actually be holding an unfortunate situation in place!

Working with the Bagua Map is one of the most powerful ways to create positive change in your life. The objects you choose act as Environmental Affirmations (page 58). When placed with intention in the Guas specifically related to the areas in your life you want to improve, the Ch'i can really move! Any one of the Ch'i Enhancers (page 37) can be used to power up Bagua areas. Just be sure you love your choice. The more personal meaning an enhancement has, the more powerful it is.

When you want to change something in your life that is mediocre, unhappy, or stressful, you may experience some chaos as a new order is being established. If you are unhappy in your marriage and decide to enhance the Love and Marriage Gua to reinstate marital bliss, the first thing you'll be faced with are the reasons you are unhappy. Working with

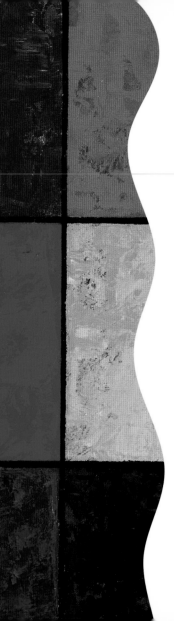

the Bagua enhances the flow of Ch'i, and the enhanced flow will push whatever is hidden out into the open. If you aspire to excellence, everything mediocre has to be cleared out first. Bringing this ancient wisdom into your household can feel like a whirlwind at first, throwing parts of your life into chaos. Just remember that when they land, they form a more auspicious arrangement. And, please be very specific about what you want, because working with the Bagua Map confirms Ram Dass's words: "Watch what you wish for, because you are going to get it."

You can map and shape the Sea of Ch'i that flows through your home into perfect harmony. Let your environment be an accurate reflection of who you are now and all that you are aspiring to be. And get ready. It's my experience that your call for positive change is always answered.

About the Author

Terah Kathryn Collins is an internationally recognized Feng Shui author, consultant, speaker, and teacher. Her first book, *The Western Guide to Feng Shui: Creating Balance, Harmony, and Prosperity in Your Environment*, is one of the best-selling Feng Shui books in the world and has been translated into eight languages. Her second book, *Home Design with Feng Shui, A-Z*, is a colorfully illustrated quick reference guide; while her third, *The Western Guide to Feng Shui, Room by Room*, contains more than 100 photographs on the subject. Terah's *Feng Shui Personal Paradise Cards* feature an informative booklet and 54 colorful flash cards that explain all of the Feng Shui basics.

Terah is the founder of the Western School of Feng Shui in Solana Beach, California, and the originator of Essential Feng Shui, which focuses on the many practical applications Feng Shui has to offer our Western culture. Featured on the PBS Body and Soul series, Terah has spoken at numerous special events, including the New Millennium Conference in Mexico, Magical Mastery and Today,s Wisdom Tours in Australia, and the Empowering Women Conferences across the United States.

For information on the author's programs, please contact:

The Western School of Feng Shui,
437 South Highway 101, Solana Beach, CA 92075
800-300-6785 or 858-793-0945
Website: www.wsfs.com

Also by Terah Kathryn Collins

Books/Card Deck

Feng Shui Personal Paradise Cards (card deck and booklet)

The Western Guide to Feng Shui:
Creating Balance, Harmony, and Prosperity in Your Environment

The Western Guide to Feng Shui—
Room by Room

Audiocassettes

Introduction to Feng Shui

The Western Guide to Feng Shui
(6-tape audio program and workbook)

Hay House Lifestyles Titles

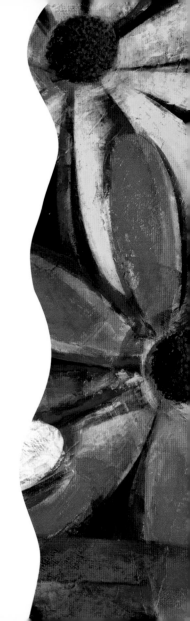

Flip books

101 Ways to Happiness, by Louise L. Hay

101 Ways to Health and Healing, by Louise L. Hay

101 Ways to Romance, by Barbara De Angelis, Ph.D.

101 Ways to Transform Your Life, by Dr. Wayne W. Dyer

Books

A Garden of Thoughts, by Louise L. Hay

Aromatherapy A–Z, by Connie Higley, Alan Higley, and Pat Leatham

Constant Craving A–Z, by Doreen Virtue, Ph.D.

Healing with Herbs and Home Remedies A–Z, by Hanna Kroeger

Heal Your Body A–Z, by Louise L. Hay

Home Design with Feng Shui A–Z, by Terah Kathryn Collins

Homeopathy A–Z, by Dana Ullman, M.P.H.

    and

Power Thought Cards, by Louise L. Hay

What Is Spirit?, by Lexie Brockway Potamkin

All of the above titles may be ordered by calling

Hay House at 800-654-5126

Please visit the Hay House Website at: www.hayhouse.com

We hope you enjoyed this Hay House Lifestyles book.
If you would like to receive a free catalog featuring additional
Hay House books and products, or if you would like information about
the Hay Foundation, please contact:

Hay House, Inc.
P.O. Box 5100
Carlsbad, CA 92018-5100

(760) 431-7695 or (800) 654-5126
(760) 431-6948 (fax) or (800) 650-5115 (fax)

Please visit the Hay House Website at: www.hayhouse.com